How to PAINT
MUSCLE CARS
& SHOW CARS
Like a PRO

Tony Thacker
with Mick Jenkins

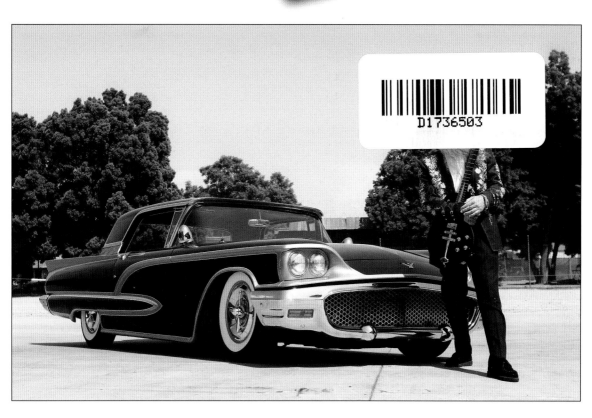

CarTech®

CarTech®

CarTech®, Inc.
838 Lake Street South
Forest Lake, MN 55025
Phone: 651-277-1200 or 800-551-4754
Fax: 651-277-1203
www.cartechbooks.com

Edit by Bob Wilson
Layout by Connie DeFlorin

ISBN 978-1-61325-413-4
Item No. SA420

Library of Congress Cataloging-in-Publication Data

Names: Thacker, Tony, author.
Title: How to Paint Muscle Cars and Show Cars Like a Pro / Tony Thacker.
Description: Forest Lake, MN : CarTech Books, [2018]
Identifiers: LCCN 2017061679 | ISBN 9781613254134
Subjects: LCSH: Muscle cars--Painting. | Automobiles--Painting.
Classification: LCC TL255.2 .T43 2018 | DDC 629.2/6--dc23
LC record available at https://lccn.loc.gov/2017061679

Written, edited, and designed in the U.S.A.
Printed in China
10 9 8 7 6 5 4 3 2 1

DISTRIBUTION BY:

Europe
PGUK
63 Hatton Garden
London EC1N 8LE, England
Phone: 020 7061 1980 • Fax: 020 7242 3725
www.pguk.co.uk

Australia
Renniks Publications Ltd.
3/37-39 Green Street
Banksmeadow, NSW 2109, Australia
Phone: 2 9695 7055 • Fax: 2 9695 7355
www.renniks.com

Canada
Login Canada
300 Saulteaux Crescent
Winnipeg, MB, R3J 3T2 Canada
Phone: 800 665 1148 • Fax: 800 665 0103
www.lb.ca

CONTENTS

ACKNOWLEDGMENTS

Book writing is primarily a solitary discipline, except when you are writing a how-to book such as this. The process then becomes one of collaboration, as you need the help, opinions, and experience of experts.

I began painting motorcycles in my parents' basement, but a friendship with Pete Darwell of Mech Spray, Britain's leading custom paint shop at the time, led to full-time employment and firsthand knowledge of the art of custom painting. This was in the early 1970s, when custom acrylic paints, primarily from

Pete Chapouris III who re-founded Alex Xydias's SO-CAL Speed Shop in 1997, was a huge influence on both Mick Jenkins and Tony Thacker. Both men worked at SO-CAL; Jenkins headed up the shop and Thacker handled PR. They both owe a huge debt of gratitude to Chapouris, who mentored them, introduced them to everybody he knew, and, most importantly, taught them all he knew.

Metalflake Corp., were just becoming available in England. There was a steep learning curve as to the great attention to detail needed to produce a show-winning finish, but Darwell turned out some fantastic paint jobs and taught me a lot. Sadly, I didn't wield a camera in those days and consequently have only memories of those early creations.

When I began writing, my second published freelance story was about custom painting at Mech Spray. The accompanying photos were not great but were taken by me using a Russian 35mm Zenit camera bought by my dad, who always encouraged me to try anything. I'm not sure that included spraying motorcycles in his garage, but he never said no.

Mick Jenkins's career took a very different, more structured path. He was schooled professionally in the body shop arts by completing a four-year City and Guild's apprenticeship in panel beating and bodywork. During these formative years, when so many good practices were developed, Mick worked at a Ford dealership and met Peter Patton, who became his friend and mentor.

Mick and myself both immigrated to the United States, me in the late-1980s and Mick in the mid-1990s, and we both owe a huge debt of gratitude to the late Pete Chapouris III. Chapouris cofounded Pete & Jake's Hot Rod Parts and went on to re-form the SO-CAL Speed Shop in 1997. Mick and I both worked at SO-CAL; Mick managed the shop while I handled the PR. Chapouris was an amazingly talented, genuine guy who introduced us to everyone in the industry and beyond and imparted every nugget of knowledge he could pass on.

While Mick was already regarded as one of the best painters around and had painted the first of three America's Most Beautiful Roadster (AMBR) Award winners, Chuck Svatos's *0032*, it was his work at SO-CAL that really put him on the map. Under Chapouris's watchful eye for detail, Mick painted everything from Jim Green's vintage front engine dragster to Billy Gibbons's *CadZZilla* to Bill Lindig's *Indy Special* that won the AMBR in 2012, Mick's second win.

The work from SO-CAL was a steady stream of top-shelf hot rods and customs, but in 2010 Mick was approached by Steve Strope, owner of Pure Vision Design in Simi Valley, California. Another transplant, this time from the East Coast, Strope had quickly built an enviable reputation as a thinking man's builder of exceptional muscle cars. Strope was looking for a new painter and Mick came highly recommended. The two hit it off, became fast friends, and scored when Strope's *Anvil* Mustang built for Matt Lazich won the coveted Ford Motor Company Design Award at that year's SEMA Show.

Strope's pure vision led to many more collaborations and awards, and this book would not have been possible had it not been for Strope's acknowledgment of Mick's talent to deliver a top-notch finish.

One friendship leads to another, and once again Mick met his customer Bob Florine, vice president of Automotive Racing Products, through Strope. Florine and Strope had a vision to build a wildly customized 1957 Ford Del Rio Ranch Wagon that would be way overpowered by a John Kaase 520-ci Boss Nine. Mick's Paint handled the entire body and paint part of the project that went on to garner yet another Ford Design Award at the 2017 SEMA Show.

Those are the major players that helped make this book happen but it would not have been possible without a whole lot of other folks who helped along the way. That list includes all of Mick's staff, who work tirelessly to make the paint jobs the best they can be and get the vehicle to the show on time. None of this would have been possible without them and they know who they are.

We have to thank contributors such as Randy Lorentzen of Planet R, Alex Maldonado of Blacktop Society, and Didier Soyeux for use of their great photography. We also have to thank Mike Cranford, who is now president and CEO of Applied System Technologies. We first met Cranford when shooting the *Great Hot Rod Build-Off* television show when he was with Patton's, and he helped immensely in designing and implementing the spray system at Mick's Paint. Cranford's contribution was invaluable as was the contribution of other industry folks, including those at PPG and FinishMaster in Ontario, who helped pull the book together.

Of course, we have to thank our wives, Anastasia Jenkins and Kailay Thacker, without whose patience, help, and encouragement this project would never have been completed. Finally, we have to thank all of Mick's loyal customers because without them, none of this would have been possible.

INTRODUCTION

It's just a paint job. How difficult can it be, right? Wrong. A poor or mediocre paint job can easily destroy hundreds of thousands of dollars and many hours invested in a project. The first thing judges see is the paint and if it's not up to par there is no way your muscle car is going to stand out from the crowd or win that coveted award.

The unfortunate thing about paint is that the uninitiated perceive it as "just paint" and not particularly difficult to do. That's because they have probably never painted a car and even if they have, they've probably never painted a car to critical show standards. When performed properly, the process is long, arduous, exacting, and expensive; it's far more expensive than most people imagine. However, as the process and cost of repairing production cars, particularly those with multistage pearl paint jobs such as the Nissan GT-R Super Silver and the Porsche GT Silver, escalates, the public is forced to become more educated about the complication and real cost of top-quality paintwork.

Earl Scheib did an incredible marketing job when he advertised, "I'm Earl Scheib, and I'll paint any car, any color for $19.95. No ups, no extras." The company is still in business and actively servicing a particular niche of the market. Unfortunately, this $19.95 figure has become lodged in our collective brains and, even though he made that claim in the 1950s, many of us still think a paint job costs less than a 12-pack. It's difficult to convince the layman that a gallon of modern water-based, eco-friendly paint now costs between $400 and $1,000 or more. That's just the tip of the iceberg. The materials alone to paint one show car can cost as much as $15,000 (and sometimes more), and that's not taking into account any of the equipment costs.

Of course, back in Scheib's heyday paint was more or less a simple one-shot operation mostly employing nitro-cellulose lacquer, known as lacquer, and you could brush it on. It was not the multilayer, environmentally sensitive process that it is today. In addition, our standards

Finished and being photographed for Street Rodder *magazine, Bob Florine's 1957 Ford Del Rio Ranch Wagon was conceived and built by Steve Strope's Pure Vision Design with body and paintwork by Mick's Paint.*

The wagon's subtle modifications range from an Art Morrison chassis up through the stretched doors to the custom trim and the Thunderbird hood scoop.

were lower. We accepted flaws such as paint that wasn't as shiny as it should have been; we just buffed it up on a Saturday afternoon. Maybe there was some overspray somewhere; maybe the door gaps were uneven. We didn't really worry too much about it. However, in today's overly critical world those flaws have become unacceptable and people expect a top-of-the-line finish even when they are not prepared to pay for it. The only time overspray is acceptable is when it's supposed to emulate factory overspray in a restoration or concours-judging situation.

Under the hood, the wagon is all muscle in the form of a stack-injected 520-ci Boss Nine. John Kaase Racing Engines built the engine, which produces 770 hp and 730 ft-lbs of torque.

To explain what it takes to paint a car to win a major award such as those handed out by Ford Motor Company at the annual SEMA Trade Show or at the annual Grand National Roadster Show, I reached out to one of the country's most talented painters, Mick Jenkins of Mick's Paint in Pomona, California. Mick's Paint has won numerous awards because Mick follows a process that he developed over the years. It's a process that he knows will get great results and last for years, certainly a lot longer than it takes you to get the car home.

When we began this project, we had intended to follow one car through the paint process and add photographs of other relevant projects to better explain the process. Our intended victim was Matt Blackmer's red 1965 Pontiac GTO. Unfortunately, as sometimes happens, the project stalled for reasons beyond anybody's control. Luckily, into the void stepped Steve Strope of Pure Vision Design in Simi Valley, California, a long-time associate of Mick's Paint. Mick has painted several award-winning muscle cars for Strope, who had an exciting project needing completion for display at the annual SEMA Trade Show.

The project was Bob Florine's 1957 Ford Del Rio Station Wagon. You could argue that the wagon is not technically a muscle car, but all doubt is removed when you open that custom hood to reveal a 520-ci Boss Nine built by John Kaase Racing Engines. Producing 770 hp and 730 ft-lbs of torque, it has muscle all right, and then some.

In addition to its awesome powertrain, Bob's wagon is loaded with subtle and not-so-subtle modifications. These include the highly modified Art Morrison chassis to reshaped and repositioned wheel arches to doors that were stretched 3.5 inches. Moreover, tailfins were added, along with 1957 T-Bird door handles and eyebrows, peaked fenders, shrunken gas door, frenched headlights, custom inner fenders, a front valance, grille and bumpers, custom trim, and the Thunderbird hood scoop.

The paint is a subtle two-tone blend of Ferrari Avorio and Aston Martin Bridgewater Bronze. It looks simple; how difficult could it be? Right? Wrong. As with all paint jobs that come out of Mick's Paint, it's what you don't see that matters, such as the thousands of hours that went into stripping, carefully sealing, priming, sanding, priming, sanding, and so on before any color was laid down. Great care had to be taken to get the color separation just right. Meanwhile, all that fragile tapered and curved stainless steel trim had to be hand-formed because of the 3.5 inches added to the length of the doors. After the paint was applied, the finished surfaces were patiently hand-rubbed. It began with 1000-grit Wetordry and working through 1500-, 2000-, 2500-, and finally 3000-grit paper to get that perfect, scratch-free surface. Of course, the trick is to never rub through. The perfect paint job takes patience, time, care, and money.

In the case of Bob's wagon, probably 2,750 hours are in the body and shaping. This is by no means excessive and it doesn't include the actual metal shaping. This is typical of what it takes to paint a car to Mick and Strope's show-quality standards. The proof, of course, came at the annual SEMA Show where, once again, the team picked up a Ford Design Award for its superb craftsmanship.

Mick Who?

Born west of London, England, Mick Jenkins completed a four-year panel beating and paintwork "City and Guilds" apprenticeship while

Mick Jenkins has spent more than 30 years in the refinishing business. He now operates Mick's Paint in Pomona, California, and is one of the country's leading custom painters. Mick poses here with his 1934 roadster. He's now working on a similar 1932 highboy. (Photo Courtesy of Alex Maldonado/Blacktopsociety.com)

serving his time at a Jaguar dealership in his hometown. Through hard work and attention to detail, he quickly attained a management position at the age of 24. Eventually, he managed a staff of 65 at the collision shop of a major Ford dealership group on England's south coast.

An avid motorsports fan, car guy, and motorcycle rider, Mick followed his dream to California in 1995 and immediately found a niche in the Southern California car culture. He opened Mick's Paint in Huntington Beach and soon gained a reputation for excellent bodywork and paint with an impressive portfolio of high-profile projects for Buick and Toyota, as well as aftermarket companies including SO-CAL Speed Shop, Budnik Wheels, Hot Rods by Boyd, Dan Fink Metalworks, and GMT. That period culminated in his collaboration with Foose Design to paint and prepare Chuck Svatos's 1932 Roadster, which won the America's Most Beautiful Roadster (AMBR) award at the 2000 Grand National Roadster Show.

In 2001, Pete Chapouris invited Mick to join the award-winning team at the SO-CAL Speed Shop as the Hot Rod and Race Car shop manager to oversee the day-to-day running of the operation. In addition, he painted a number of customers' cars, including Gene Olsen's 1950 Merc' convertible, Jim Green's *Assassin* Top Fuel dragster, Billy F Gibbons's 1958 Thunderbird *Mexican Blackbird*, Dennis Higginbotham's *Spencer II Roadster*, and Bill Lindig's blown Ardun Deuce Roadster, which was featured in the popular international TV show: *Hot Rod Build-off*.

In 2010, after re-forming Mick's Paint, Mick became associated with Steve Strope of Pure Vision Design and painted the 1969 *Anvil* Mustang that won the Ford Motor Company Design Award at the 2010 SEMA Show. That car heralded the beginning of an enduring relationship with Strope that has resulted in more

This 1958 Thunderbird, Mexican Blackbird, was built for ZZ Top front man Billy F Gibbons at the SO-CAL Speed Shop and painted by Mick's Paint. While it's not a muscle car, it does show the versatility of Mick's work. (Photo Courtesy of Alex Maldonado/Blacktopsociety.net)

Mick's first collaboration with Steve Strope's Pure Vision Design resulted in the 1969 Anvil Mustang that won the Ford Motor Company Design Award at the 2010 SEMA Show. The 520-ci Boss 429-powered car was built for Matt Lazich of Anvil Auto to showcase its line of composite parts. (Photo Courtesy of Didier Soyeux)

In 2012, Mick's painted the 1965 Martini Mustang; Steve Strope's Pure Vision Design built it for Karl Williams. It won the Ford Motor Company Design Award at that year's SEMA Show. (Photo Courtesy of Didier Soyeux)

Ed Pink Racing Engines built the highly detailed engine of the T5-R Martini Mustang: a 1960s-era 292-ci DOHC Ford Indy V-8.

The Halo 1972 TT Camaro, built by Steve Strope's Pure Vision Design and painted at Mick's Paint, won the GM Design award at the 2013 SEMA Show.

Powered by a 1,400-hp twin-turbo 427-ci small-block, the 1972 TT Camaro was a badass, long haul ride built for Ron Lallo.

Another Pure Vision and Mick's Paint collaboration was this 1967 Ford Fairlane built for Ed Chalupa. It won the Ford Motor Company Design award at the 2014 SEMA Show.

A 521-ci all-aluminum SOHC big-block Ford engine built by Ed Pink Racing Engines powers the Black Ops 1967 Ford Fairlane.

Mick had a hand in painting these two wildly flamed Freightliner Optimus Prime trucks. They were used in the Transformers movies and also for promotional activities.

Yet another Pure Vision Design/Mick's Paint joint effort was this 1968 Charger built for Karl Williams. It appeared at both the 2013 and 2014 SEMA Shows. (Photo Courtesy of Didier Soyeux)

than a half-dozen extraordinary muscle car builds.

Not one to let an award go to his head, Mick and his team of highly skilled craftsmen continued to turn out exemplary work. Among these are cars for Billy F Gibbons of ZZ Top that included a repaint of the famed *CadZZilla*. He also painted the 2012 AMBR winner, the Indy V-8 Speedster for Bill Lindig. Later that same year, the Pure Vision 1965 *Martini* Mustang owned by Karl Williams won the Ford Motor Company Design Award at the SEMA Show.

More awards followed: The *Halo* 1972 Camaro won the GM Design award at the 2013 SEMA Show, and the 1967 *Chalupa* Fairlane won the Ford Motor Company Design award at the 2014 SEMA Show. At the 2012 SEMA Show, the *Martini* Mustang garnered an award from Mothers while Lindig's Indy Speedster picked up two more awards from Mothers.

Meanwhile, Mick began working with Mickey Larson of Twins Custom Coaches, assisting in the build of a fleet of custom-painted show trucks for Freightliner and Western Star. That fleet included a pair of *Optimus Prime* trucks for the *Transformers* movies.

Mick's Paint, however, is not confined to the hot rod, custom, and muscle car world. Mick has painted everything from a Porsche Speedster and a 1958 Pegaso Z-103 that came third in its class at the Pebble Beach Concours d'Elegance to a rare 1931 Alfa Romeo 1750 Spyder and a 1941 Packard four-door convertible. There was also a 1955 Alfa Romeo Boano that won its class at the 2017 Pebble Beach Concours d'Elegance, as well as several Ferraris, a lightweight E-Type Jaguar, a "hot rod" concrete pump, a pair of background walls at

Amir Rosenbaum of Spectre Automotive had this 1970 El Camino built at the SO-CAL Speed Shop before Mick's Paint handled the mile-deep black paint. With a setback LS7 engine, it was featured on the TV show **Hard Shine**. (Photo Courtesy of Alex Maldonado/Blacktopsociety.com)

The engine in Amir Rosenbaum's Spectre El Camino SS was an LS7 Corvette Z06 set back in the chassis and built for the Optima Ultimate Street Car challenge. (Photo Courtesy of Alex Maldonado/Blacktopsociety.com)

Disneyland, a semitruck covered in chrome-plated nails, and a few motorcycles.

Most recently, and due to customer demand, Mick's Paint has expanded its capabilities into full builds. This includes everything from frame-off restorations to complete frame-up builds. Mick's third AMBR Award came at the 2017 Grand National Roadster Show with Bruce Wanta's amazing 1936 Packard Roadster.

A complete, ground-up build by Troy Ladd's Hollywood Hot Rods, the *Mulholland Speedster* featured a handcrafted steel body with a retractable, cantilevered hardtop. Mick's Paint handled the body and paintwork. The car won the AMBR, as well as the America's Most Beautiful Custom Award, the Sam Barris Award, the Custom D'Elegance Award, and the World of Wheels Legend Cup in Chicago.

Later that year at the Annual SEMA Show, Bob Florine's 1957 Ford Del Rio Ranch Wagon, built by Steve Strope's Pure Vision Design and painted by Mick's Paint, garnered another Ford Design Award.

In a little more than 20 years, Mick has reached the top of his game but, as he is quick to point out, you are only as good as your team. He also warned that you should never stop learning. New paint materials, technology, regulations, and, most important, new projects, keep you on your toes.

This 1969 Camaro Convertible has been in the same family since 1970, but a multiyear, multishop restoration resulted in many lost parts. However, Steve Strope's Pure Vision Design and Mick's Paint returned it to its former glory.

The engine compartment of the Camaro is testament to the work of both Pure Vision Design and Mick's Paint. It never looked like this from the factory; at times in its life, it has looked a whole lot worse.

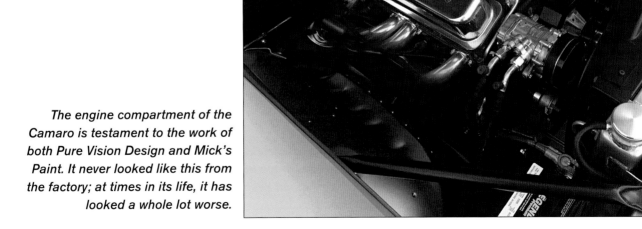

MAKE A PLAN

As Ben Franklin said, "If you fail to plan, you are planning to fail!"

The logic behind this book is to share our experience, expertise, and technical knowledge with anybody who is game enough to want to undertake tackling the body and paintwork on their own muscle car project. What we have to share will be of benefit to anyone wishing to restore or even just repaint a car. The person who will gain the most will be the one who knows the least going in. Nevertheless, we're certain that anyone who reads this will pick up some useful tips for the long and often arduous road to restoration.

This is one business in which you never stop learning because the technology and regulations are constantly changing. If you think you know everything there is to know then you are way too smart to be working and playing with cars. As this book was in its final stage of preparation, we had an incident where a painter had moved to California from another state and he was unused to painting with water-based materials. Despite being instructed on the prevailing methods, he insisted on painting, in particular mixing, in his tried and true way.

Unfortunately, those methods don't work with these different chemicals that typically require a lot less reducer. Needless to say, he mixed his paint and painted the car only to find that his old methods were redundant. The whole car had to be rubbed down and started over. No matter what you think you know, read and follow the instructions.

In this book, we'll concentrate on process and technique rather than the chemical aspects of paint materials or legal requirements. You can study the wide variety of materials that are available as well as the legal requirements regarding refinishing in your city and state or country through books and the Internet. Mick's Paint is located in California, where the maze of regulations is very confusing. You could call two different paint stores and get three different answers.

Regardless of what you are painting, whether it's a muscle car, a hot

Find a car such as this 1963 Dodge 880 with decent factory paint and you should think very seriously about keeping the original paint. A repaint might alter the value significantly.

rod, a custom, a truck, a motorcycle, or whatever, the principles are the same and those principles are what we will be covering in this book. First, you need a plan. You need to know how long it's likely to take, how you are going to get 'er done, and, most importantly, how much it's going to cost.

Of course, you can ignore all this and plough ahead, but in our experience not knowing what you're in for is a prelude to disaster. Forewarned is forearmed. For example, if you get the body prepped and had not accounted for the cost of paint materials, how are you going to finish the project? You can't leave it in primer, as primer typically absorbs moisture. You won't notice for a few months but that moisture works its way down to the steel where it initiates oxidation. A year in and you're going to have to strip the car back to bare metal, including all the Bondo. It makes sense, therefore, to have a plan and know what you're getting into.

To Paint or Not to Paint

To paint or not to paint is a question that you might be wondering why we're even asking, but if you have an original muscle car with factory paint then you have to consider carefully whether to paint or not. Even if the paint is worn out and flat, sometimes on the right car original factory paint is what you want; it adds value when a repaint might devalue the car.

If the factory paint is good in places but bad in others, you have to review it thoughtfully and see if the damaged or badly worn places can be repaired without painting the whole car. Again, it might save you time and money and result in a car that is worth more than if you had repainted it.

Once the decision has been made that a complete, down to bare metal paint job is required, it's time to do some further thinking. The first thing to be aware of is that a quality finish is not a job for the faint of heart. It will take you weeks or months if not longer to complete. Some of the top-level jobs at Mick's Paint have in excess of 1,000 hours of labor. That's 25 weeks, equaling half a year, and that's for a professional; an amateur may take even longer. This is time-consuming work with few shortcuts. That's why top-notch, show-quality paint jobs cost so much. If or when you uncover some less-than-satisfactory repairs under the existing paint, it will be depressing and probably more expensive than you budgeted for.

What Car to Paint

Of course, you might already have the car of your dreams, the car you want to restore and repaint rusting in the back 40, cozy in a garage, tarped in the driveway, or, worse, rusting in the yard. However, if you don't have the car and you're trying to figure out what car that should be, read chapter 4 that goes into the decision-making process more fully. Be aware, though, even at this early stage in the process, a poor decision now will no doubt turn out costly in the end.

Are Parts Available?

I'll get into parts sourcing in more detail in chapter 4, but, again, even at this preliminary stage you want to be thinking about where you're going to get any parts you might need. If a 1971 Pontiac GTO convertible is your dream car, we can tell you that the parts are expensive and difficult to locate.

Mick's Paint recently had one in the shop that needed some bodywork, including a new hood. After weeks of searching, a used hood was found for $3,500 but it looked rusty

This pair of tidy Mustangs is in great shape and therefore may be too good and original for what we have in mind. However, it pays to buy the best car you can that is together and complete with all its trim and pieces. A body shell with a pile of parts is not the way to go. Worse still, in Mick's opinion, is a car in primer.

This 1971 GTO convertible turned into a problem. A good original hood was impossible to buy so a fiberglass hood was sourced. The headlight surrounds are original fiberglass.

A hood for this 1965 El Camino shouldn't be difficult to find because, after all, it's interchangeable with the Chevelle. The problem is that all the good ones are on Chevelles, consequently making them not easy to find.

The GTO's original Endura front bumper was so bad that it needed to be replaced with a fiberglass piece that can be massaged for a better fit.

How Much Will It Cost?

in the photos and needed shipping across the country. By the time it was shipped, was acid dipped to make sure all the rust was removed, and was prepped, it would have cost the customer at least $5,000 before paint, and that was the cost if it didn't need any other bodywork, which you know it would have. In the end,

the owner opted for a good quality fiberglass hood, as the car was not a restoration.

Maybe your dream car is a 1971 GTO, which is a rare car worth restoring, something like that might be out of your price range. It might be time to think about a more popular car to tackle for your first big project.

People who don't know much of anything about painting cars are always surprised at the time it takes and the cost it involves. "It's just paint. How can it be so expensive?" Well, things have moved on since Earl Scheib painted cars for $19.95 and materials are no longer inexpensive. A gallon of paint in Los Angeles is now between $400 and $1,000 a gallon depending on the color, with reds being more expensive. If it's a metallic or pearl base coat and clear process, then you're going to need clear coat. A good quality clear coat costs $450 a gallon and you'll need three to four gallons. Why so much? Well, you want it to look good and you want plenty of clear so that you don't sand through to the actual color.

To paint the outside of a typical muscle car might take as much as four to five gallons of paint alone if you go the single-stage route, not including inside the trunk, under the hood, and other miscellaneous areas.

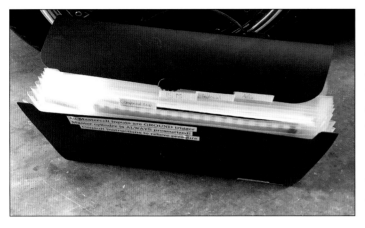

Totaling up the costs may scare you, but you should keep a file of all paperwork and invoices related to your project. Proof of what you spent could help you retain the value of your car.

If you use the two- or three-stage approach, the amount of paint will be less, maybe 2.5 gallons, but you're going to need a similar amount of clear coat as well as the relative reducers, hardeners, and so on.

You're also going to need to buy more than you need so that you have some left over for the inevitable repair. If you are intending to paint under the hood, inside the trunk, and those other areas, then you are going to need as much as four gallons. Remember also that you should put aside a quantity of paint in case the one you choose goes off the market for some technical or regulatory reason that is beyond your control. If you have to make a major repair then you'll be glad you saved some paint.

You should also be aware that some colors cover better than others and for the ones that don't cover well, you're going to need more. Mick's Paint always gets way more than needed, just in case.

Something else to be considered carefully is the quality of the materials you select. There are cheap materials on the market; for example, you can buy some clear coats for $150 a gallon compared to good clear coat at $450 a gallon. But, we have had many experiences where that cheap clear coat deteriorated within a year

to the point that all the paint had to be stripped off, including the base coat, and we had to start over. Some cheap paints contain no Ultra Violet protection and fade quickly, causing deterioration. Consequently, the apparent initial savings are far outweighed by the eventual costs of redoing all that work. Buying cheap materials is false economy.

In addition to the cost of the actual paint, there are ancillary materials to purchase, such as stripper, which you will need one to two gallons of at the cost of $46 a gallon. There's also metal prep, sealer, primer, body filler, sanding discs, masking tape and paper, clear coat plus the necessary activator and reducer, rubbing paper, polishing mops, and compound, to name a few. The list goes on and on.

These days the cost of materials alone can be $5,000 or more. That's just your out-of-pocket costs. That's not including all the hidden costs such as tools, equipment rental, booth hire, etc., which you have to factor in.

How Long Will It Take?

How long is a piece of string? In the case of a good quality paint job, much longer than you think. There really are

no shortcuts to a good, long-lasting, quality paint job. In Mick Jenkins's opinion, a top-quality finish typically consumes 1,000 hours, at the minimum. In the case of a show-quality paint job, you can double that figure and then add some. Keep in mind that 1,000 hours equates to 20 50-hour weeks. That's more or less five months, if you can put in 50 hours a week. If you're only working weekends and the odd evening and you're working alone, this project is going to take half a year or more, maybe a year. Be prepared for the investment of time as well as money.

I know, you've seen the TV shows where the car is painted in a day. So it can't take as long as I'm saying, and perhaps the actual spraying could take as little as a day but usually it takes about 30 working hours to properly apply paint. TV shows are not reality; the work is shown in a compressed time frame to make the work of many hands fit into a one-hour time slot. Do not believe what you see on TV. It is not reality.

If spraying only takes 30 hours, where is the rest of the time going, you ask. Prep work is where all the time goes. Without the requisite prep work, you will not enjoy the fruits of your labors. The paintwork will not be as good as you'd hoped for and you might have to start over. Consequently, figure you're going to invest 1,000 hours, probably more if you get the car down to bare metal and find that it is far worse than you anticipated and you have a lot of repair work ahead of you.

How Much Space Will I Need?

For the most part, muscle cars are big. Our GTO project measures 17 x 6.3 feet. Even a pony car such as

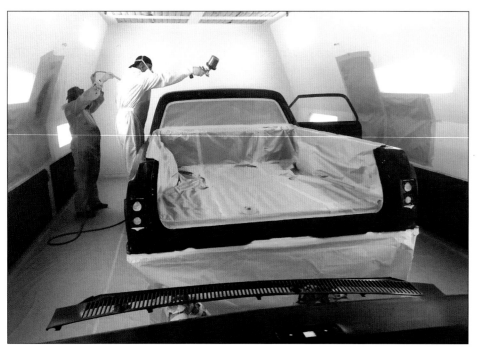

You're going to need a fair amount of working space to accommodate a muscle car. Ideally, you need room to open the doors, accommodate the removed parts, and allow one or two guys to move around the space. Mick's Paint's booth measures 30 x 15 feet.

a Mustang measures almost 16 feet long and 6 feet wide. You are going to need a good-sized garage in which to work around the car. A 20 x 10 is really too small. Mick's Paint's booth measures 30 x 15. Of course, you can do the prep work outside if that's your only option, but be thoughtful of the mess that tearing apart, stripping, and sanding a car makes. Rubbing down water makes a mess that is not easy to clean up from a driveway unless you have a power washer.

Besides the space to work on the car, you're also going to need space in which to store and prepare parts. For example, if you remove the hood, decklid, doors, or the front fenders, you need a place for them to be spread out. A good-sized workspace is therefore a must.

It's important, in Mick's opinion, to remember that in a professional environment the spray booth is for just that, spraying. It shouldn't really be used for anything else because of potential contamination. Treat it like an operating theater and keep it clean.

Where Will I Paint It?

Good question. Where will you paint it and, just as importantly, who will paint it? If you want a really good job done, you're going to need to paint in a booth. And if you have no experience, you're going to need a painter.

You have, I hope, a circle of friends who can give you some direction about who to trust in your area. A lot will depend on where you live and the network you have in the surrounding locale. While working on some projects in Portland, Oregon, I found only a limited number of resources for auto restoration, builds,

upholstery, paint, etc. It was quite different from a big city such as Los Angeles, where there appears to be an endless supply of shops.

When there are many shops to choose from, it is important to do your homework. Not all shops are to be trusted, and you really need to get some references from past customers. Talk to those customers at car shows and other gatherings. Get their opinions, especially a year after the work was performed. Ask how it is holding up, but remember that there are always three sides to every story: their side, the other side, and the truth. All opinions have to be taken with a pinch of salt. Somebody who disses a paint shop may have run out of money or balked at the price and that could be the reason for the falling out, not a bad paint job.

Caveat emptor, "buyer beware," is always the watchword. You're about to spend a lot of hard-earned money on this project, so now is not the time to make a hasty wrong decision.

If you're planning to tackle this project in a friend's shop or garage, be very aware of the time factor. Many years ago, I was invited to take my car to Keith Baker's body and paint shop, thinking my project would only take six months. Two years later I was still futzing with it. Thankfully, we didn't really fall out and we are still friends but two years is a long time in somebody's shop where they could be earning money with the space you are occupying.

In large cities, such as Los Angeles or Detroit, you can rent a booth. Prices vary across the country, of course; however, during my research I found that prices ranged from as little as $150 a day at Rent-A-Paint Booth in Gresham, Oregon, to $300 a day in Detroit. Rent-A-Paint Booth

My local Earl Scheib painted this 1966 Mustang coupe for a reasonable $2,500. However, the owner had to strip or mask the trim. The owner had a choice of color and Scheib warranties the work for three years.

Inflatable paint booths such as this one from Carcoon America can provide a space where you can paint your project.

An unanticipated expense might be the cost of renting an enclosed trailer to move your vehicle to and from the paint shop. Trailering a masked or freshly painted car on an open trailer is not recommended.

will also allow you to leave your car overnight to dry and pick it up the next day. And, while they don't have a painter on site, they can recommend one.

Don't be fooled into thinking that you're going to paint your car in only one day and will only have to pay for one day's rental. You're not Earl Scheib. Typically, a competent masking job will take most of a day. You could do the masking somewhere else but unless you transport the car in an enclosed trailer the car

and the masking is going to get dusty and that dust can ruin your expensive paint. Remember, it's $1,000 a gallon. Transport is another cost to factor in, especially if you don't own a truck and trailer and have to rent one.

It's going to then take you at least a day, but more likely two days, to paint your car. It's a big job, there's a lot of paint to apply, and you probably will not be able to paint it all at once. Mick's Paint usually paints the roof first, if there's a convenient split

such as a piece of trim, as there are on 1960s cars. However, later cars such as Camaros and Mustangs have no convenient break and the car has to be painted in one go. Then there are those panels you removed that need color on both sides. There's no way that those can be done in one day. Keep in mind that you might not be able to fit the car and the panels in the booth all at the same time. To be on the safe side, Mick recommends that you rent the booth for four to five days minimum, preferably a week to be on the safe side. Add that to your budget.

Unfortunately, after calling dozens of listed rental operations, I found that many no longer offered booth rental services. They quoted customer abuse of the facility and equipment as their reason for terminating the services.

Another option, assuming you have or can find the space, is an inflatable booth from companies such as Carcoon America in Jacksonville, Florida. Carcoon manufactures inflatable workstations in a variety of sizes that are like bounce houses with windows. You can use one of these to work on your vehicle. They come in a variety of sizes, are EPA Certified, and also meet and exceed OSHA ventilation and NFPA combustible material requirements. It's certainly an option.

Who Will Paint It?

Who will paint it is another question you should ask yourself early on in the planning stage. If you have no experience whatsoever, it's probably advisable to come to terms with the fact that you're not a painter and you're going to need help. My dad owned a construction company and always instilled in me that a person could do anything if he or she put his or her mind to it. It helped to know a few tricks of the trade. He was probably right and, consequently, I've tackled many projects that I had no training for, including body and paintwork, but I have come to understand that spraying is not my forte and I need help.

If you plan on using a solid color with no metallics or pearls, you could paint it yourself using the knowledge gained from reading this book. However, if this really is going to be your very first attempt at painting a car, we strongly suggest that you not only study this book but also seek help elsewhere. Different opinions are always good. You could even sign up for paint and body classes if they are available in your area. There's no substitute for experience, so if you do nothing else, get ahold of a spray gun and practice.

If you are uncomfortable tackling the paint, then you will obviously have to either take it to a paint

You can find good painters in the unlikeliest of places. Albert De Alba Jr. of Cal Blast is one heck of a painter. Note: He did not paint this 1960 T-Bird in his blasting shop; he painted it elsewhere.

shop or hire a painter. If you take it to a paint shop, unless you know the owner/painter very well, expect to be shown the door. Why? Because the painter is unlikely to want to put his name on the paint when he has no idea how you have prepped the car. For all he knows, you primered the car with spray bombs over whatever was there before. He'll paint it and before you can say *reaction* there could be, well, a reaction that is possibly going to have repercussions for the painter. People will think it's his fault that the paint reacted when, in fact, your prep will have been the cause.

One possibility that we've heard of is to contact your local one-day paint specialist and see if its painter would be interested in painting your car. All they do is paint all day long, so they have to be experienced painters; maybe there is an opportunity for you to do the prep and have them handle the paint application. That is, if it's not too complicated.

Unless you have a good painter

in your back pocket that trusts your work and is prepared to paint over your base, there is no simple solution to finding a painter.

What Equipment Will I Need?

The tools and equipment needed are outlined in more detail in chapter 3. Needless to say, it's everything from hammers and dollies all the way through to a suitable welder. The list is much longer than you think possible, but if you're a crafty, hands-on person then you might already own most, if not all, of the tools required to complete a showable restoration or custom. We have listed here some equipment that only professionals are likely to have.

Body Dolly

You will need some items such as a body dolly if you remove the body from the chassis. You can make a body dolly or you can buy one. You might even be able to rent one but

If you're planning a full body-off restoration, you will need to figure a body dolly into your plan. You can build your own or purchase one from a company such as Best Buy Automotive Equipment.

If you're going all the way and taking the body off the frame, you must fabricate a simple tube structure to prevent the body from twisting. It's cheap insurance.

think of the time this project will take, a year at least, and realize you don't want to be renting a dolly for a year.

Rotisserie

The same goes for a rotisserie. It is best to budget for one if you are going the full monty. If you are tak-ing the body off the frame then you will need to construct a steel tube structure to help hold the body in shape and prevent it from flopping over. Of course, this structure should be fabricated before you remove the body from the chassis and while you still have the doors in place. You might also want to consider other

Because of its size, the support structure for Bob's wagon was substantial. It included a central cross frame to hold the body in shape as well as other supports, such as these on the doors.

If the budget allows and you intend a full restoration, you may opt for a rotisserie such as this one from Auto Lift; however, they cost around $1,000. You can find used rotisseries, but be sure to get one that can support the weight of your body.

You may also need dollies to support fenders, the hood, and other take-off parts including the decklid and doors. Remember to put the dollies on wheels.

Rendering

A rendering is an image or model of what you want the finished product to look like. It is something else to consider before you dive into a project, not so much a restoration but certainly a custom paint job. Having a rendering done gives you a road map, even if it's only a guide, that will help keep you focused.

As you can see, there's a lot to plan when it comes to tackling a professional level paint job for your muscle car. One of our first steps when starting a new project is to make a checklist of all the things we have outlined above. Then, determine a ballpark figure of what the project will require in regard to both time and cost. Unless you have done this before, you will be surprised at the amount of time and money necessary to achieve above average results. You will no longer question the paint shop when they quote you time and materials.

structures to hold fenders and the hood, as they might make it easier for you to work from.

Ideally, all of these work mates need to be on wheels. Also keep in mind where you are going to store them both when they are in use and not in use, as they do take up a lot of space.

A rendering can run somewhere between $300 and $1,000 but having a vision of what you want your project to ultimately look like is money well spent. It gives you a road map, a destination, and inspiration when energy is lagging. It can also generate some publicity, if that's your goal, and it's a very cool thing to have framed for the man cave. Steve Stanford created this rendering of Ed Chalupa's 1967 Ford Fairlane. Steve Strope's Pure Vision Design built the car and Mick's Paint painted it.

We were able to follow the build and painting of Bob Florine's 520-ci Boss Nine–powered 1957 Ford Del Rio Ranch Wagon. Steve Stanford rendered it and Steve Strope's Pure Vision Design built it. It looks like a simple two-tone paint job, but you will see that it is complicated when you want to get it right.

TOOLS AND EQUIPMENT

As you saw in chapter 1, Make a Plan, you will need some specialized equipment that is not generally found in the toolboxes of most home mechanics. At this point, you might need to pause and once again ponder if this task is for you. It's not that sanding blocks, hammers, and dollies are expensive, but grinders and spray guns can be; a good gun can easily cost $1,000. These items may be a one-time investment, and you have to ask yourself if that investment is worth it. Are you ever going to do this again? If the answer is no, then I would seriously consider having a professional shop tackle your bodywork and paint.

Something else to consider is that metal can be tricky stuff. It reacts. Hit it with a hammer and it stretches. Shrinking it back to where it started is by no means easy; it's one of those tricks of the trade my dad told me about. Likewise, rust only looks easy to remove. Heck, you just cut it out, but replacing a panel or even a quarter panel is not a task for the inexperienced. You can certainly learn as you go, but you have to ask yourself if this is the project to learn upon. Inexperience can actually create more problems than what you started with. The result will be that you end up having to go to a body shop anyway. You might as well have gone to a professional in the first place. It is important to know your limitations and come to terms with them.

If this is a path you want to take because you want to learn, that's great. If possible, get a panel from the same car or at least the same era and practice on that before you begin. Bash it. Hammer it. Heat it. Shrink it. See how the metal reacts and responds to your input. If you put a dent in it, can you persuade it back into shape? In the old days, a body man would spend years doing an apprenticeship, as Mick did, learning his trade and honing his skills. Don't think that you're going to become a professional overnight from learning on just one job or from a YouTube video. Patience is the name of the game. You can't be in a rush; remember, more haste less speed.

If you find you need to replace a panel, and find a reasonably priced match, be aware that replacement panels don't always fit as you hope they would. Sometimes, they barely fit where they touch. They could, therefore, need a lot of work, if not major surgery, before they align properly.

What You Need

You've decided to move forward. That's great! Obviously, a lot of the equipment you will need can be rented from your local auto body shop or from places such as The Home Depot and other rental facilities, but be aware that these tasks invariably take much longer than anticipated and planned for. You have to plan accordingly, knowing that what you thought would take a day will undoubtedly take two or more. The extra days will cost more and that will affect everything you do in each step afterward. As we have said and will say over and again, all this needs to be thought through and planned for.

Stripping Equipment

Mick prefers W.M. Barr's Aircraft Paint Remover from Klean Strip. Other products are available including aerosol options. However, if a non-fluorocarbon option is available, I prefer that to an aerosol. Besides the actual stripper, you're going to need a slew of associated products including mixing cups, brushes, scrapers, bucket, Visqueen (a brand of polyethylene plastic sheeting) to protect the floor, and masking tape and paper as well as the aforementioned safety gear. You'll also need a couple of workstands on which to support any removed panels.

Chemicals

It's amazing how many chemicals you will need to complete the whole restoration process. The list includes: cleaners, degreasers, adhesion promoters, Quick Check, Guide Coat, etc. These items are explained in chapters 9, 10, and 11.

Masking Tape & Paper

Some shops appear to use whatever is on hand to mask a car, but any old tape and paper just doesn't cut it. If you're on a budget, you might be inclined to use newspaper or something similar for masking, but it's really not a good idea. For one thing, newspapers are thin and the paint can bleed through. Also, there is the possibility that the ink can "print" on to your paint job; it's not a desirable effect. Professional masking paper is treated to prevent the penetration of paints and solvents. It is available from auto body stores in a number of widths from 4 to 36 inches wide. How much you will need will depend on the size of the car and the extent of the project. For the full-on project chronicled in the painting chapters, we used six rolls of paper.

You want the tape to work to keep the paint away from the surface, but you don't want it to be so sticky that it is not easily removed. Some cheap tape that is super sticky can be useful where the better and less sticky tapes do not adhere; for example, when trying to tape over Body Schutz (3M Branded undercoating) or something similar. There are many brands and types of masking tape available, but Mick prefers to use 3M Scotch 233+. It is available in a number of widths, resists solvents (something non-automotive grade tapes do not), can withstand 250 degrees Fahrenheit for 30 minutes, and is available from numerous outlets including ULINE and any auto paint store.

Masking Station

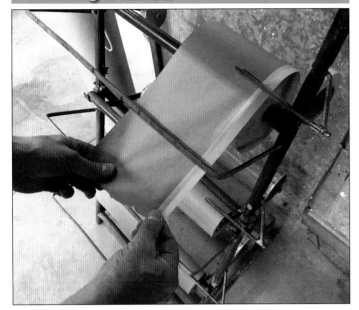

To make masking easier and more efficient, Mick uses this masking station that facilitates the application of masking tape to paper. Similar stations are available from companies such as Astro and Eastwood. Single stations are also available from 3M, Easy Mask, and Shurtape.

Workstands

Mick uses lightweight, portable, tubular workstands because they are easy to move and fold away when not being used. Similar stands that hold up to 750 pounds are available from Eastwood. Note that Mick wraps his stands in masking paper to prevent overspray build up on the legs and especially the padding.

Safety Equipment

Paint materials are generally regarded as dangerous, even the water-based materials, so the more you can do to protect yourself and the environment throughout the process is very important. We know of too many painters who have suffered health problems from years of unprotected exposure to solvents. You never see anybody in Mick's paint booth who is not protected from head to toe with coveralls, gloves, and spray mask. Yes, this adds a layer of expense, and perhaps inconvenience, to your task but what's your health worth?

If you want to protect your health, a powered, belt-mounted air-purifying respirator such as this one from 3M will prevent you from inhaling any solvents. They can cost $1,500 or more.

Oil and Water

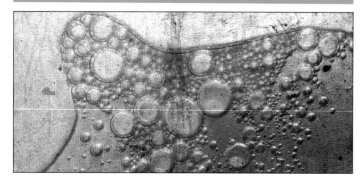

Oil and water do not mix and are especially not good mixed with your paint. Because of the heat generated by compressing the air, water vapor will inevitably build up in the compressor lines. This is especially the case if your tank is too small and the compressor has to work too hard, heating up the air and generating moisture. Be sure to use plenty of filters to eliminate contamination.

Primer Gun

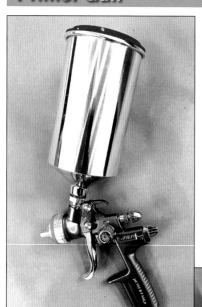

Mick uses this SATA Jet 100 BF HVLP low overspray primer and filler gun exclusively for primer.

For high-build primer such as polyester primer, Mick uses a nozzle size of 2.1. He typically uses larger nozzles or tips for this part of the job, as they work best for thicker materials.

Spray Guns

There are numerous spray guns on the market. Even if you are only going to spray one car in your life, a quality spray gun is essential. A good online source to look at the many options is AutoBodyToolmart.com. A quarterly printed catalog called Auto Source Today is also a good source that is available from most auto body stores. However, we recommend making friends with your local auto body paint store and purchasing locally. The local shop is more likely to help you when you have questions or problems, and you will have one if not the other.

High Volume Low Pressure (HVLP)

It used to be that most common guns had the paint cup on the bottom and worked via siphon; however, those old guns were extremely wasteful and are now illegal. Consequently, new high volume low pressure (HVLP) guns were developed to help reduce the amount of wasted paint and resultant pollutants. The HVLP gravity fed guns have 30-percent better transfer efficiency than the old siphon guns. They are more efficient because many use a disposable cup complete with a filter that slips inside the paint cup. Sure, there's waste but it is a far more cost-effective system. ■

Color Gun

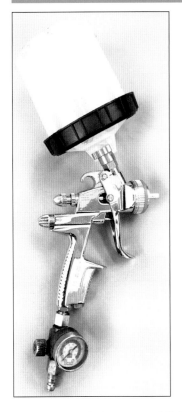

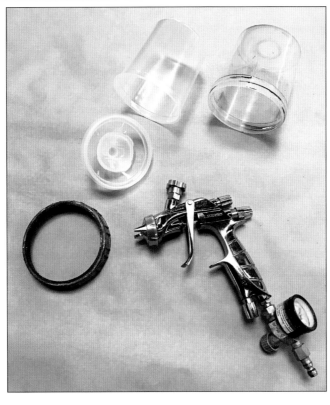

You can see here (left) how the paint cup breaks down into its component parts consisting of the cup (with blue tint), the liner next to it, and the filter below.

For color and clear coat, Mick prefers the SATA 3000 B HVLP (top left). Note the pressure gauge in the airline and the easily removable clear paint cup that accepts disposable paint cups for easy, quick cleaning.

For most color applications, Mick uses a nozzle size of 1.4. The stainless paint needle and nozzle make it suitable for water-borne paints, for which a 1.25 nozzle is used.

Detail Gun

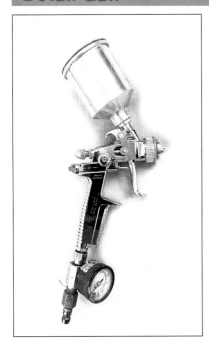

Automobiles are tricky things to paint. Even though the outside is big and kind of flat, there are all sorts of nooks and crannies that are inaccessible with a conventional gun. Therefore, a professional will have a smaller detail gun that he can use for doorjambs, tight corners such as those in a pickup bed, and other tight areas. Prices vary with quality.

Gun Cleaning Brushes

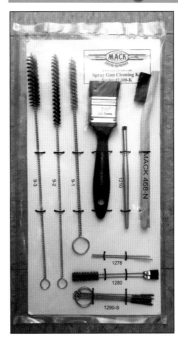

Andrew Mach has this 15-piece brush cleaning kit that is essential for keeping your spray guns clean. Other kits are available in a range of costs.

Schutz Gun

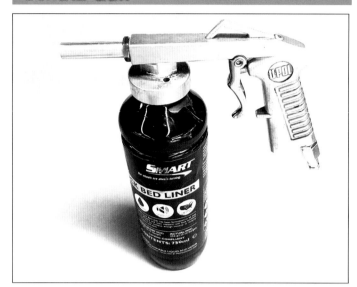

If you're planning on addressing the underside of your project, you're going to need a Schutz gun, such as this lightweight one from U-Pol, to apply the material.

Hammers and Dollies

If metal bashing is anticipated then you are going to need some specific hammers and dollies. Of course, some of these tools can be found used at swap meets, at garage sales, and on the Internet. Here are some of the metal shaping tools in Mick's drawers. Eastwood offers a similar seven-piece hammer and dolly set that includes three hammers, a toe block, a heel block, a general-purpose block, and a light dinging-spoon for less than $100.

Other Tools

You're going to need an orbital sander, also known as a dual-action (DA) sander, as they rotate and orbit. The larger the pad size and the wider the orbit or offset, the larger the surface area you'll be able to work at any one time. However, one size does not fit all jobs; you're going to have to pick a size that works best for you. Mick's preference is for the air-powered DAs, preferably with vacuum, as they are more reliable and cost effective. They reduce dust if a collection bag is attached; though, you'll need perforated backing pads and sanding discs, otherwise the vacuum is irrelevant. Note that you will need a compressor of at least 5 hp with at least 4 to 5 cfm at 90 psi to run one tool at a time.

Vise-Grip (Locking Pliers)

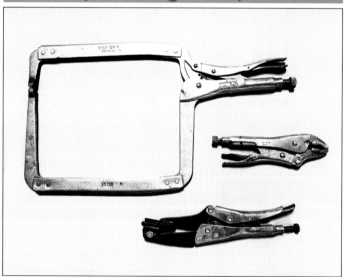

You will need an assortment of locking pliers. These come in various sizes and you probably won't know what you need until you get the paint stripped. The larger versions for bodywork are known as locking C-clamps.

Sanders and Buffers

For detail polishing, Mick's Paint uses either the battery-operated, well-used Snap-On CTPP761 (left) or the air-powered Dynabrade (right). Both companies make a wide range of auto and body shop tools.

Mick prefers an air-powered dual-action (DA) sander. They produce a swirl-free finish. This particular model is from Snap-On and does not have a vacuum attachment.

Mick's Paint uses this Makita 9227 7-inch, variable speed (from 0 to 3,000 rpm) electric polisher. It has a preset speed setting dial (from 600 to 3,000 rpm) for maximum control. Most buffing is done in the 600 to 1,500 rpm range.

A die grinder is another handy tool that will help you clean those difficult-to-get-to places such as drip rails. They're best if they are air powered but electric and even cordless ones are available from manufacturers such as Makita. Mick uses an air-powered Wurth 1/4-inch Angle Head No. 111957.

Sanding Discs

You're going to need a selection of sanding discs to use with the various sanders and grinders. The discs are available from local and online paint suppliers.

Sanding Blocks

Amateurs tend to use their hands as sanding blocks, but your hands are not flat and, despite what you think, they can leave small, finger-shaped grooves on the surface. Professionals, on the other hand, use a variety of sanding blocks, many handmade, to affect a flat surface. These blocks can be as simple as a sandpaper-wrapped paint stick or as complex as professionally or custom-made long blocks that work on large flat surfaces. Remember, when using long blocks always use both hands to evenly spread the pressure. Using one hand in the middle of a long flexible block will only work the center of the block, wasting your time when you are trying to achieve a flat surface.

Sandpaper

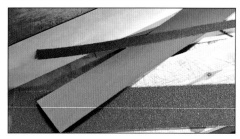

You won't believe how much sandpaper of various types you will go through when repainting a complete car.

Dry paper is used for the initial sanding stages to remove old paint, cut back filler, and so on. This paper would be in the range of 40-grit being the coarsest to 220-grit being the finest used on body fillers. You can see here that the body guys have cut the paper into more versatile sizes.

3M Wetordry paper is used for flatting back during the various color sanding stages starting with 800- or 1000-grit and

going all the way to 3000-grit paper if you follow the 3M system. You can go to 3M's site and learn all about it at 3M.com/3M/en_US/total-automotive-sanding-system-us/.

Wire

Mick uses rebar wire to tie parts to the various hanging frames he employs. Available from Lowes, The Home Depot, and other home improvement stores, rebar wire is strong and flexible. It can be used again and again without breaking.

You will be surprised at how many components you will need to hang to paint. You could, of course, use old wire coat hangers to hang them.

Jacks & Axle Stands

You probably already own a jack and some axle stands, but if you don't you will no doubt need to add them to the list. They will come in handy.

Creeper

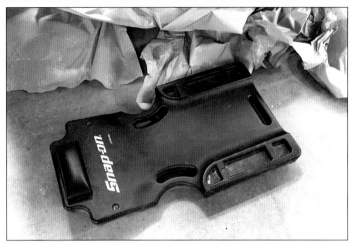

A creeper is always going to come in handy around the shop. Mick uses them to look under cars that he's thinking of buying. He also uses them when sanding or masking the undersides of cars to be painted.

GoJaks

GoJaks might seem like an extravagant luxury at around $200 each, but they are invaluable when trying to move vehicles in tight, confined spaces such as paint shops. If you plan to do a lot of this work, they are well worth the investment.

Wet/Dry Vacuums

A wet/dry vacuum will also come in handy around the shop. We prefer the Rigid Wet/Dry offerings, as they are robust and long-lasting tools. We just said good-bye to one after 25 years of trouble-free use.

Sand Blaster

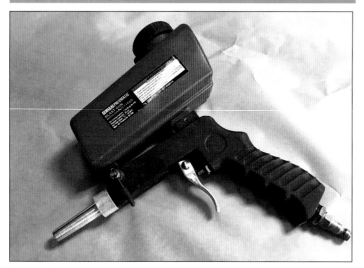

A small gravity-fed sand blaster such as this one from Central Pneumatic/Harbor Freight Tools can be very handy for small jobs and removing rust from small pit holes.

Blow Gun

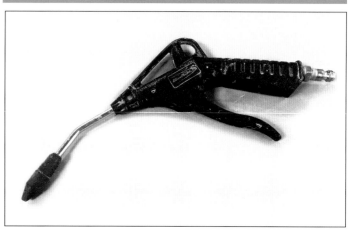

A blowgun with a rubber tip or rubber tip attachment is ideal for blowing things dry and for cleaning out any blasting debris. This one is available from Snap-On. Mick also prefers them for blowing dust from a clean-ish car before applying quick detailer.

Auxiliary Lighting

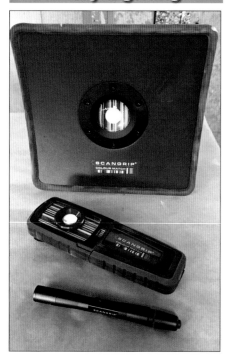

Auxiliary lights are used for color matching and illuminating the surfaces to check for small pinholes and scratches that might later cause a problem. This selection came from Scangrip.

Welder

For general purpose welding and bodywork, Mick uses this Miller Dynasty 200 tungsten inert gas (TIG) welder. It can be used to make precise welds when joining mild steel, aluminum, or stainless steel. TIG welding is a two-handed process (one hand holds the torch while the other feeds filler metal) and it commonly involves a foot pedal or fingertip remote to control the arc voltage while welding. Like MIG welding, a shielding gas (typically argon) is required.

Manuals

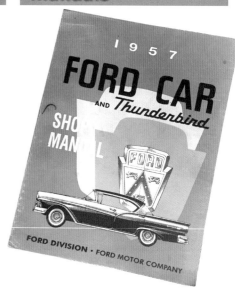

The best shop manual you can find is also an essential tool in the restoration or rebuild of your project. Obviously, a lot of information is online, but sometimes it's good to have a book in front of you.

Compressors

By Mike Cranford, President and CEO, Applied System Technologies

When selecting an air compressor for painting a vehicle, some of the most important factors to consider are the pressure requirement (psi) and air consumption (cfm) of the spray gun, as well as the available horsepower. Air consumption is measured in terms of cubic feet per minute (cfm). Most spray guns used for painting vehicles feature relatively low consumption, in the range of 7 to 15 cfm. For example, a 2-hp air compressor delivers approximately 7 cfm, while a 3-hp compressor produces about 10.5 cfm.

A good choice for a small one-man shop or home garage would be a 5-hp two-stage reciprocating compressor that delivers around 16 to 18 cfm at 175 psi. This will provide adequate cfm and psi for most air tools while allowing you to use a point-of-use pressure regulator at your spray gun to reduce the pressure for painting. The compressor should have a minimum of a 60- to 80-gallon air receiver (tank) for air storage. These compressors are available online and at many home improvement and tool stores, but you may want to consider buying from a professional supplier that provides service and parts such as Patton's.

A new compressor of the correct capacity is going to cost upward of $1,000. We checked out a Quincy model, PN 2V41C60VC, at Lowe's. The 60-gallon 175-psi two-stage electric air compressor with a 5-hp motor meets the requirements. The cost was $1,299. Similar is an Ingersoll Rand SS5L5 that also costs around $1,300. Of course, you can also find used compressors online at machinery supplier sites such as MachineryTrader.com. Beware of buying without any type of guarantee, as repairing a compressor can be costly.

Once you have chosen a compressor, you are going to need to remove the moisture in your air system to prevent paint contamination. One of the best methods to eliminate moisture is to use a high-temp refrigerated air dryer along with a coalescing filter placed at the inlet side of the dryer to remove any oil carryover from the air compressor followed by a particulate filter at the discharge side of the dryer to trap any fine particles that may enter the air system.

The compressed air system at Mick's Paint is a Patton's system that separates the shop air from the air supplied to the paint booth. The regulations for painting vehicles in California require that all paint be of the waterborne type. For this reason Patton's employed an oil-less scroll air compressor dedicated solely for the paint booth. This particular scroll

This Quincy Compressor PN 2V41C60VC 60-gallon, 175-psi two-stage electric air compressor meets the requirement with its 5-hp motor. You can order it through stores such as Lowe's. (Photo courtesy Quincy Compressor)

Something similar is this Made in the USA compressor from Polar Air by Eaton. This one is from its Whisper series. It features a single-phase 5-hp motor and an 80-gallon tank.

compressor technology uses no oil for lubrication, eliminating any possibility of oil from the compressor contaminating the paint. Patton's also used a duplex oil-lubricated reciprocating compressor system for the shop air that assured more-than-adequate cfm and psi required to meet the shop's needs. Both systems were supplied with proper drying and filtration to assure a clean and dry air system.

One of the most important and overlooked aspects of the compressed air system is the air piping. At Mick's Paint, Patton's used an aluminum pipe system with nickel plated brass push-connect fittings. This is an all-metal system with no plastic or polymer fittings called Infinity; it is manufactured by Applied System Technologies.

Compressors *continued*

Infinity piping offers the performance of heavy, traditional steel piping at the cost of systems using plastic. Its revolutionary lock-and-seal design ensures a totally safe, leak-free system for all compressed air, vacuum, and inert gas applications. The solid brass, nickel-plated fittings make the system easy to use and install. Infinity's powder-coated aluminum pipes are so light that they can be handled and installed by one person. There's no welding, gluing, or threading; a simple pipe cutter and de-burring tool are the only tools required. ∎

The compressor system at Mick's Paint was created specifically by Patton's to separate the shop air for tools from the air supplied to the paint booth. This particular scroll compressor technology uses no oil for lubrication, therefore eliminating any possibility of oil from the compressor contaminating the paint.

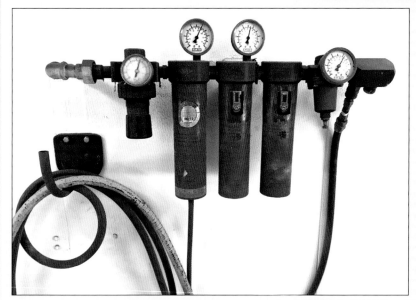

This bank of filters at Mick's Paint prevents any contaminants from the compressor systems from entering the airline to the gun. Note also that the hose is wrapped in masking tape to prevent any old overspray stuck to the hose from falling off into the paint. The masking tape is changed out for every job.

Powermate Air Tools Approximate CFM Requirements

Tool Type	Req. CFM	Tool Type	Req. CFM	Tool Type	Req. CFM
Angle Disc Grinder	6 cfm	Dual Action Sander	6 cfm	Ratchet 1/4 inch	3 cfm
Air Drill 1/2 inch	4 cfm	Grease/Caulking Gun	4 cfm	Ratchet 3/8 inch	4 cfm
Air Drill 3/8 inch	4 cfm	High Speed Grinder 5 inch	4 cfm	Sand Blaster (3 gallon)	4 cfm
Butterfly Impact	3 cfm	Impact Wrench 1/2 inch	5 cfm	Spray Gun (commercial)	6 cfm
Chisel/Air Hammer	4 cfm	Impact Wrench 3/4 inch	7 cfm	Spray Gun (HVLP)	18 cfm
Cut Off Tool	4 cfm	Nailer	1 cfm	Straight Line Sander	7 cfm
Die Grinder	8 cfm	Orbital Jitterbug Sander	6 cfm		

BUY THE RIGHT CAR

Buying the right car is always the right decision. Buying the first example you find of your dream car, especially if it's cheap, is almost always a mistake. Buying the wrong car will almost certainly cost you dearly in the long run. Believe me, we've all done it.

Over the years, I've seen more than one grown man reduced to tears when his dream machine is torn down and the paint is removed only to find a rusted out, beaten up, poorly repaired, patched together heap of tin.

Panel Debate

When searching for the right car, keep in mind the availability of replacement panels. Mick Jenkins has had any number of situations where a customer has had a car stripped only to find rusted-out panels that are not readily available, if at all. You wouldn't initially think that is possible, but if a car was a low-production model that didn't sell and wasn't popular when new then chances are that the few cars that were produced were scrapped when folks moved on. Fast-forward 50 years or more, and original muscle car panels can be exceedingly difficult to find, expensive when found, and maybe not even in the greatest of shape.

Mick's Paint had one customer with a 1971 Pontiac GTO convertible that had a rotted out hood. Mick searched all over for a replacement hood, and the only one he could find was equally rusty. The price was $3,500 plus shipping. The customer ended up using a fiberglass hood, reluctantly.

We recently looked at a 1965 El Camino that needed a full repaint. While doing our due diligence, we found that tailgates are very difficult to find, no surprise there. Equally difficult to find are doors, rear quarter panels, and the hood. The hood is the same as a Chevelle and, consequently, is difficult to find because

You might pass on this 1969 Dodge Dart at first glance, but a closer inspection reveals that it's in good shape. Although the paint is faded, it's actually original. There's no visible rust, and the trim is all there. This might be a good candidate for restoration.

Before you buy your dream car, research the market and see what parts are available and what they cost. Remember, just because a panel is available that doesn't mean that it's going to fit easily. It is most often the opposite case.

the Chevelle owners have all the good ones.

This situation reminded Mick of a 1969 Camaro convertible that came into the shop. It had already been to two shops but still wasn't right. The first shop claimed it had "lost" the doors, the front fenders, and the convertible top. It's difficult to lose such bulky items accidentally. Possibly they were sold because they were valuable. The second shop had purchased cheap reproduction replacement panels. When the fenders were stripped, it was obvious that

Trans Am

This 1970½ Pontiac Firebird Trans Am was my dream car. Unfortunately, under all the custom paint and molded-in factory flares, it was a bit of a rust bucket. Of course, I was right to want to restore it. After all, they only made 3,196 of them.

My dream 1970½ Pontiac Trans Am was one of those nightmare cars. A friend owned it, and I loved it. Loved it too much to see through the flaws that were obvious to everyone but me. For starters, the factory flares had been molded into the body and it had been custom painted. The molded flares should have been warning enough, but I ploughed on and handed over my hard-earned money. I bought it with the intention of putting it back to stock. After all, they only made 3,196 of this model. It was an investment. They're worth money now.

I took the Trans Am to a friend with a body shop for advice. That advice was, "Sell it." I ignored him and ploughed on. Reluctantly, he agreed to help me and we stripped the car to bare metal. I should have listened to him.

The Bondo-repaired molding of the flares disguised the fact that the plastic factory parts were all ripped and torn. The molding around the flares was likewise ragged. The bottoms of the front fenders, the doors, and the rear quarters were all rusty as was the panel between the rear window and the decklid, a notorious rust spot on those early 1970s GM cars.

Too late now, we were down to bare metal and I had to buy the rear panel and the factory flares. They were not cheap. I also had to patch the bottoms of the doors and the quarters. I was devastated by the amount of bodywork necessary before I could even begin the repaint. Thankfully, my friend, whose advice I should have taken, helped me through the process.

Once finished, with paint complete and expensive factory decals applied, I had it hauled home on an open trailer. Sadly, the seat belts blew out of the windows and hammered the new paint down to bare metal. I had to have it repainted, again. What had initially appeared to be a simple restoration had turned into an ongoing nightmare. And, it got worse before it got better. ∎

the quarters were not correct but the shop had made them fit with 3/4 inch of Bondo to align them. The Bondo had to be chiseled out and new quarters installed. This discovery resulted in a major delay in the project's schedule and, of course, a completely unexpected cost. All this after the customer had already wasted money at two other shops.

Rust

As you are searching for the right car, also keep in mind that early Mustangs are prone to rust in the cowl area under the dash, especially around the heater plenum, the floor pan, the trunk, the wheelwells, and the fronts of the doors. The shock towers also suffer from fatigue cracks and rust. But, all of these panels are readily available, making for easier restoration. In fact, complete, brand-new 1964 through 1970 body shells are available from Dynacorn.

Early Camaros are similarly prone to rust at the bottoms of the front fenders, where water and debris collect. In addition, the rear quarter panels rust around the wheel arch and behind the wheel opening. Early Camaro upper dash panels are often rusted at the base, where they tuck under the bottom of the glass. The rear cowl panels also rust because the rear screens are poorly sealed and there is no drain tube. The rear unit-body frame rails often rust from the inside out. They are repairable, but keep in mind the high cost in time and materials.

Many early muscle cars had vinyl tops, but buyers should beware that they may have been used to cover up rust. When buying a car, it's not possible to tear the top off to take a look, but it is important to be aware

of the problem and that it was used as a cheap fix-to-sell option.

When researching your ideal muscle car restoration project, be sure to research what parts of the car in question are susceptible to

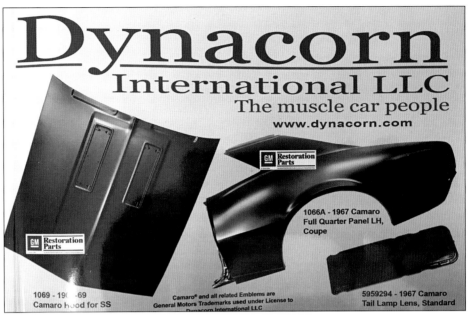

Dynacorn is one of many companies that produces replacement panels for muscle cars. It is the one that Mick prefers.

Mustangs are notorious for rust in the bottoms of the doors. This car showed only superficial rust and nothing to worry about except the trim that would need replacing.

At first glance, this 1969 Mustang Fastback looked very rough. Closer inspection revealed a surprisingly rust-free, desirable California car that could be restored to its former glory.

This Mustang sat out in the weather, and its vinyl top did not look so good. You can see that it's lumpy below the tear. Water has probably gotten in there and caused some rust.

Farther up there are more worrying signs of neglect. Missing trim and more tears in the vinyl that could have allowed water to seep in and cause rust.

There's a lot going on with this forlorn Mercury Cougar XR7, but at least you can see the metal

The carpets were obviously shot, but lifting them revealed that the floor pan was not rusty and still had some of its original factory paint.

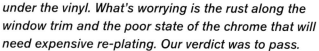

under the vinyl. What's worrying is the rust along the window trim and the poor state of the chrome that will need expensive re-plating. Our verdict was to pass.

Another area to check is the trunk area where the carpet and insulation are. The carpet and insulation was ragged in this example, but the actual sheet metal was sound.

On many cars from the 1960s, the panel below the back window allowed water to gather under the trim. Rust can rot away the panel and the sub structure. This is an example of a panel that looked good.

rust. Then check to see what, if any, replacement panels and parts are available. Also, be aware that even if panels are available it is by no means a guarantee that they will fit and/or align.

VIN Numbers

During your search for a car, a vehicle identification number (VIN) check might help you make a smart decision. That's not to say that those numbers aren't sometimes tampered with. With the right muscle cars commanding high prices, it's not beyond some unscrupulous sellers to adjust things to make a ho-hum car more valuable.

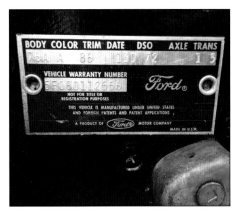

As a point of reference, it's good to check the door plate. In the case of a Mustang, it will provide body type, color, trim, date, district sales office (DSO), axle, and transmission information. Don't be alarmed if there is no plate, but be pleased if there is one and things look copacetic.

Trim Pieces

Before deciding which car to buy, you should do some research on trim pieces. Older cars from the 1950s often had stainless steel trim that, even if damaged, can often be repaired. Later muscle cars from

the 1960s might have had chrome, anodized aluminum, or even plated plastic trim that might not be repairable or available.

Damaged and dented stainless steel trim such as that on this 1960 Chevy wagon can often be carefully repaired by some gentle hammering and polishing. Worst-case scenario, it can be remade in brass if a replacement is not to be found.

Bumpers

Bumpers of that era can also be a problem. While some bumpers remained chrome steel, others did not. For example by 1968, the Pontiac GTO featured a plastic Endura nose cap and no real bumper. By 1973, U.S. Federal Motor Vehicle Safety Standard Number 215 mandated that: "1973 model year bumpers must be

strong enough to prevent headlights, taillights, fuel system components, and other safety items from damage after a 5 mile-per-hour frontal impact and 2.5 mile-per-hour rear impact." The 1973 fuel crises did not help the chrome bumper brigade.

Just imagine, it's 1968 and you're watching TV when a sharp-dressed John DeLorean appears with a brand-new, red 1968 GTO and a huge pry bar. Then, almost without warning, he slams the front bumper of the GTO. You expect all sorts of damage but, despite numerous blows, the bumper remains intact.

In his book *Pontiac: The Complete History, 1926–1986*, Thomas Bonsall says, "The Endura bumper was one of the great styling innovations of all time because it permitted stylists to blend the bumpers into their frontal styling. Until it came along, front bumpers usually had the look of having been added to a design, rather than being an integral part of it."

Within a few years, other Pontiac models followed suit. It wasn't long until plastic bumpers were fitted to the Camaro. They were even added to the Barracuda and Challenger, where they were known as the Elastomeric bumper.

Again, in your search for the holy grail of muscle cars, be aware

Even chrome-plated steel bumpers can need repair or modification to create a custom fit. They will also need stripping and re-plating, which can be expensive.

This early-1970s AMX grille has it all going on as well: chrome, stainless steel, and plastic. If you had to find or repair one, watch out. The car has poor hood alignment too, but that issue was common and not too difficult to fix.

Beware the Endura and similar plastic bumpers of the 1970s and 1980s. They are around 50 years old now and have suffered the ravages of time. They didn't fit great when they were new and they're not adjustable to modern standards. Although not original, a fiberglass replacement is Mick's preference for these bumpers.

that plastic bumpers were exposed to sun and heat. Those bumpers on cars from the Southwest or from California tend to deteriorate quicker than others, but nearly all suffer from cracked paint or actual cracks in the plastic after a while.

Regardless of the regulations, repairing or even remaking chrome bumpers can be fairly simple compared to trying to repair or, heaven forbid, fabricate an Endura assembly. The other problem with Endura-style bumpers is that they are not adjustable. What you have is what you've got. The factory fit was pretty sloppy and in today's world that's usually not good enough. Consequently, Mick's Paint prefers a fiberglass replacement for the Endura bumpers that can be built up or sanded down to align with the adjacent sheet metal.

Be wary when looking to buy a car with chrome bumpers as well. They can be deceptive, too. They can look great from the front but they can be almost rusted through from the back with just the chrome holding them together. And again,

Rick Lefever had to use four sets of original trim to make two pieces of trim for Bob Florine's 1957 Ford Del Rio Ranch Wagon. Try finding four pieces of good original trim for a 1957 wagon even if a little more than 46,000 of them were made.

The 1960s' cars had it all: stainless steel trim, anodized aluminum headlight buckets and grille bars, chrome insignia trim, and chrome steel bumpers. If replacement parts arc not availablc, it will takc a talented metal man to make the necessary repairs.

as with the trim, you might have to cut up more than one bumper to fabricate the shape you need. The cost and difficulty of chrome plating can be prohibitive, especially if the pieces have to be shipped to and from a good chrome shop.

Be aware that what applies to panels, bumpers, and trim, applies equally to many other parts of the automobile. There can be difficulty replacing glass, rubber seals, the dash, and the wiring, for example. I recently had to look at a car that somebody in England wanted to buy. It looked pretty good on the Internet, but personal inspection revealed many of the parts, including all the dash, thrown in the trunk. How would I ever know if it was all there or not? My advice was to pass.

Another overseas friend imported a car found on the Internet only to discover that the "other" side of the car, the side not shown in the photographs, was almost completely missing. This is shared to remind you to only buy a car that you have seen and inspected firsthand; it is the only sensible way to go.

All this is not to say that a few difficult-to-find parts should dissuade you from pursuing your dream

A good friend owns this 1971 Chevelle and freely admits that it's a "back East" rust bucket with semigloss black paint that hides many holes and much Bondo. However, since moving West it has miraculously become a "California car."

car; that's not the case. It's just that at this stage in the process you should be aware of the often unforeseen difficulties ahead and factor the realities into the workload and the projected budget.

Do Your Research

Muscle cars of the 1960s and early 1970s might well be the last American automobiles that can be restored with a wrench and a screwdriver. After that, there was too much molded plastic, too many wires, too many relays, and, eventually, the addition of computers that make the restoration process difficult at best and impossible at worst.

Consequently, do your research. Read the books, especially the marquee histories available from CarTech, as they provide a wealth of knowledge about muscle cars and their idiosyncrasies. You can also search the Internet, where there is almost too much information. You can also talk to experts who may be willing to give up their knowledge to help you make the right decision.

In summary, go with a pessimistic mind and a friend. If you have

Some of the Chevelle's problems are quite obvious, such as these nicely erupting blisters on the rear quarters. Again, if you can see it you should imagine what is going on below the surface. This rust will not be an easy fix.

The Chevelle had more deep cracking just behind the rear window. You know this one is not going to be pretty when the paint is removed. Note that the panel below the window had already been replaced, but what goes on below that? And, look at the rear window. That's going to need some work.

Careful inspection of the Chevelle revealed some telltale signs of rust in the lower rear quarter panels. As Mick says, "If you can see the tip of the iceberg believe that there's more below the surface."

No Primer, Please

Here at Mick's Paint we would never buy a project that is in primer. For that matter, Mick would never take on a paint job over somebody else's primer. Why? Because primer spells trouble. What it could mean is that the previous owner planned a restoration but once the vehicle was stripped he or she found either too much rust or too many repairs or excessive damage that was beyond his or her capabilities. Consequently, a quickie repair and the whole car was primered so that you, the buyer, didn't focus on the one or two repaired areas. Then it was declared ready for paint. Not so. The same goes for trendy semigloss color that can easily hide a multitude of sins, just like the same gray primer.

A good or, in this case, a bad example was a 1955 Chevy Nomad. The customer thought he couldn't afford a finished car so he purchased a project in primer, too excited to check the car out properly. The car was sent out for blasting and returned a mess. The lower quarter panels were overlapped onto the badly corroded originals, tacked on, and filled over. The roof was rotted out along the drip rails on both sides and it also needed inner and outer rocker panels, door skins, and a couple of floor pans to finish it off. The car was in really bad shape and the owner was devastated. The big question then is, what do you do now? Do you cut your losses and scrap the car or dive in and finish the project? Believe me when I say that this scenario happens more than you think. I know, I've been there and done that myself. You get excited by a new project and look beyond the lipstick and don't see the pig underneath.

There is another issue with primered cars and that is that you didn't do it. Therefore, how can you possibly know if the work under the primer has been done correctly? Worst case scenario, you prepare and paint the car on top of the existing primer that you didn't apply and have no knowledge of, you do the final assembly, and a couple of months later the paint begins to blister up from under the primer where it wasn't prepped properly. You are looking at a complete disassembly and a strip and repaint.

Another reason not to use a primered car is that you don't know what materials the previous primer used. The primer might be completely incompatible with the paint system you have planned to go on top.

Trust me, it's just not worth buying a car in primer. In our opinion, it's better to buy a car in bare metal than it is primer. ■

Camaros are cool and plentiful, but there's a lot going on with this 1969 Z28 that should make any smart buyer beware. For starters, it's in various shades of primer, which should be a huge warning sign. And let's not forget to mention the rusts spots.

It really doesn't warrant a closer inspection, as even from a distance there's too much stuff that looks frightening. First was the rust in the decklid that wasn't just on the surface; though, the decklid can easily be replaced.

It got worse as you looked lower. The panel had taken a beating, and you can see where holes had been drilled to pull it out. There's rust and there's a questionable fill of the marker light. The back panel doesn't look any better.

This Nova is a whole different bag of worms. The amateur should obviously avoid this one, but it will get repaired.

At the very least take a jack, a flashlight, and a magnet when you go to inspect any car that you might purchase. If the seller is not happy with you poking around the car, definitely be prepared to walk away. He or she may have something to hide.

This 1968 Mustang was actually a nice car and a good place to start; however, we did notice a couple of things that would give us cause to look a little closer.

As you can see, there was some misalignment of the hood. In some cases, this could indicate some poorly repaired accident damage. That was not the case with this car, though.

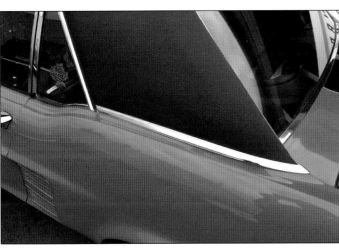

The vinyl top on this Mustang was in great shape. If you were going to be repainting the car, the top could save you money because you wouldn't have to paint it.

One thing we did notice on this otherwise clean car was the etched glass. It was a big trend in the 1980s, but etched glass is not so popular now. Replacing all of the etched glass pieces could be expensive.

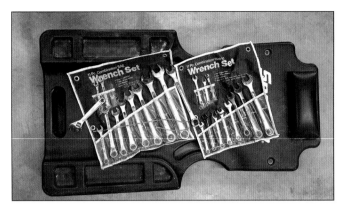

If you have them, take a creeper and some tools to check out a potential purchase. Even if you don't care to poke at the frame and floor pan, at least you can get down and take a good look at the underside.

the choice of a car from a dry state or country, that's the best place to start; however, some sellers have been known to truck in out-of-state cars in order to jack up the price, so be on your toes. Personally, if the goal is to restore the car myself and I can find one with original paint, or most of it, even if it's burnt off in the sun, I'd take it every time over a finished paint job or, worse, primer. At least it will be in honest condition with no hidden secrets and you'll know pretty well what it's going to take to complete the task rather than the unexpected quarter panel and trunk floor replacement. Again, *Caveat Emptor*, "Buyer Beware," is the phrase to remember.

Walk On By

When you go to look at a vehicle for possible purchase, first, be prepared to walk away. Yes, you might have wasted time and money to view it, possibly traveled a long way, but think of all the time and money

you'll save when you buy the right car and not the first car. Next, be prepared to get dirty as you crawl under it with a flashlight to push and poke at the inner rockers, frame rails, and floor pans. If you see rivets, screws, or signs of non-factory welding, beware. Lift the carpets on both sides, back and front, and in the trunk. In fact, check it all out thoroughly.

Run your hands around the insides of the wheelwells and check for signs of corrosion or repair. Pull away interior trim panels and look and feel inside the quarter panels where they join the rocker panels and floor. Look behind the wheel arches where they meet the inner panels.

Poke around inside of the front fenders for corrosion and repairs. The top front eyebrows of many muscle cars suffer from rust; it may also appear behind the front wheels at the lower section of the fenders. Years of holding moisture off of the front wheels will usually mean rust out or blistering paint.

If you can see blistering on a

panel, it's only the tip of the iceberg. That blistering is only the beginning of bigger things that translate to more expense. The optimist in you will immediately think, *oh, its no problem, it's just the corner of the door that's blistered*. A door is a perfect example. Up until the 1980s, most cars were not rust proofed or sealed on the insides of the panels; you were lucky if you got paint. Water inevitably snuck by the original weather strips and, with the help of gravity, found its way to the very bottom of the door. There, it crept along the seam and began to corrode the skin or flange from the inside out. Yes, you only found blisters in the corner but the real rust is a late bloomer and hasn't emerged yet.

Eventually it will break through and, worse than that, you are going to unknowingly help it. You grind or sand around the blisters that you can see but all you are doing is making the sheet metal thinner, which in turn, helps the corrosion on the inside break through quicker. Worst of all, these hidden problems usually only become evident once you've completed your repair job and the blistering appears next to the area you repaired.

Just as an iceberg is mostly below water, always assume that the rust you see on the surface is only the tip of the iceberg. What you can't see below the surface is at least twice as big. What that means is a lot of repair work or a complete panel replacement for total peace of mind.

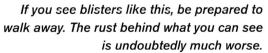

If you see blisters like this, be prepared to walk away. The rust behind what you can see is undoubtedly much worse.

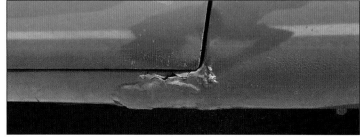

We must stress that it was NOT this Mustang, but we did look at one to purchase that was actually two cars welded together. As always, buyer beware.

Take a Friend

Mick recommends taking someone along when you go look at a car, if only for an extra pair of eyes and an unbiased opinion. Moreover, if this is for a full-on restoration project it might be worth paying for an expert opinion. The small cost could save you thousands of dollars, not to mention years of grief, gray hairs, and spousal abuse.

A funny example is that while compiling this book Mick and I went to see a Mustang for a friend in the United Kingdom. We both looked at it only to realize that it was two Mustangs welded together, which not even the seller realized. Obviously, we passed but not everybody will be so lucky.

A Tall-Order Mustang

In the middle of this book project, Mick Jenkins was asked by an overseas customer to find him a nice Mustang that was reasonably priced. The shipping and import fees to his country of residence, which can be as much as the asking price, could make the project prohibitively expensive. Therefore, he had to find a car that was reasonably priced and was also a good base for a restoration project.

That's a tall order, as good, original Mustangs command a high price. This was one of several cars we looked at. Even though it had been modified, it appeared to have great bones and proved an ideal candidate. It was the opposite of the one we found that was actually two different Mustangs joined together. ∎

At first glance, you might walk past this customized 1965 Mustang with faded paint but, despite some issues, it's a genuine 4-speed GT so worth further inspection. Turned out to be a restoration project.

A Tall-Order Mustang *continued*

Despite some rust and a few nonstock parts, the factory hood scoops and the Ford badges were all in place as was most of the trim, making this a good project.

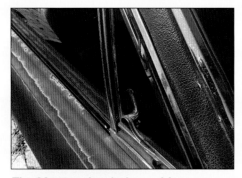

The Mustang's window rubbers were shot, but that is an easy and inexpensive replacement. Some of the trim was good and some was not so good, but overall it was not beyond repair.

Inside the cowl air intake is a prime place for rust but this example looked reasonable. However, it should be noted that this was a lifelong California car.

The original grille had been swapped for billet aluminum bars and the chrome front bumper had been replaced with this fiberglass aftermarket "fat lip." Even with those modifications, a return to stock would be an easy fix.

You can see the window rubber is shot here and will need replacing. The dash pad was also curled up from the heat. However, the window trim is actually in good shape and salvageable.

The early Mustang door trim plate is not as fancy as the 1966 plate; nevertheless, it reveals the car's basic history. Note: The color code 8 indicates that the Mustang's original color was Springtime Yellow and not the maroon as found. Therefore, it had been repainted at some time. The DSO was Houston, Texas, and the final No. 5 indicated that it was a 4-speed car, although it had been converted to automatic at some point.

The original badges were there and in reasonable shape; however, the bottom front of the door was rusted through. That's common on Mustangs. Luckily, new doors are just $200.

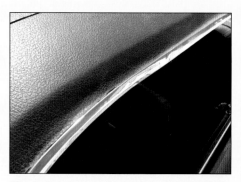

The rain gutter trim was not in such good shape, but that would be fairly easy and cheap to replace. The vinyl top did not appear to hide any really scary problems.

Overall, this 1965 Mustang turned out to be worth the time it took to check it out. Sure it would need a repaint, but we were looking for a factory 4-speed GT that was sound, original, and worth restoring.

TEAR DOWN AND PAINT REMOVAL

Every person reading this will have a different budget, schedule, and expectation of where they want or can go with his or her project. Needless to say, the key to a good paint job and its longevity is like most things and that is starting with a good foundation. Working over the top of anybody else's paint job or worse, primer, is like playing Russian roulette with a loaded gun. It will end in tears.

Tear down always seems like the fun part when you can, well, tear into it. But you should take time to disassemble your project carefully. Photograph it as you go, and save all the clips and parts that you don't know if you will need. Right now you should assume that you might need them. Don't throw anything away until the job is complete. You never know when those parts may come in handy, even if it's for checking dimensions on a new part that doesn't fit or for back-up parts if your supplier doesn't follow through. They may even become parts you might have to salvage because you have found they are just not replaceable.

For example, you might need to match the top of an existing fender to a new bottom. The rear quarter panels of a customer's GTO convertible had to be repaired because new quarters were not available and neither were used ones. The tops that had been retained and stored were matched to new coupe bottoms. It was the only possible fix.

Take plenty of photos of the engine bay if you plan on removing the engine. Also take photos of the running gear, plumbing, and electrical. In fact, shoot as much detail as you can; it costs you nothing and possibly saves you lots.

It's also a good idea to bag parts separately. Photograph, bag, and label parts from each panel as you go. Reusable plastic bags are great for holding small parts. Keep each separate and clearly labeled. For example, put left door parts in one bag and right door parts in another.

Once you have removed all of the parts that are bolted to the body, you can begin the stripping process. It's time to get messy.

Disassembly is a good place to start and extremely important to the end result. Begin by taking as many photos of your car as you can. This is relatively easy now with excellent cell phone cameras. Remember to download those photos onto a computer, hard drive, or thumb drive to keep them safe because it might be a year or two before you need them.

You should consider very seriously keeping a logbook of the hours you spend and the tasks you complete as you do them. It will provide an invaluable record and a useful reminder when you need to recall something later.

Documentation and Disassembly

1 Begin with overall view photos of the car so that you will be reminded of not only how it looked and what a great job you've done but also where parts went.

2 Photograph as many details as possible, including trim placement and, where possible, the method of attachment.

3 Photograph and carefully store items removed, such as these trim clips. If you're missing some, add them to the list of parts needed. It's tedious to only remember them at assembly time.

4 Photograph plenty of detail shots of the engine compartment and engine accessories, especially if you plan on pulling the engine. Detail photographs will be invaluable come assembly time.

5 *This shot is meant to scare you and remind you to be sure to photograph the wiring and routing. A year from now you will never remember where it all went but photographs will help. A good wiring diagram will also be useful at assembly time.*

6 *Take plenty of photographs of the instrument panel as well. Photographs of how it looks and how it came apart will be a helpful reference when it comes time to start reassembly. Notice the windshield is masked on the inside with cardboard to prevent damage to what might be rare glass.*

7 *Don't throw anything away until the project is complete because you never know what you'll need. Door lock mechanisms, window regulators, instruments, in fact, anything and everything might be of assistance when it comes to assembly time. Label everything so that you know where each piece goes.*

8 *Remember to photograph the running gear, plumbing, and electrical. It all looks simple now but in a year or two you won't remember where it all went.*

Documentation and Disassembly *continued*

9 On this GTO project, the heater is going to be replaced with air-conditioning. While the heater will not remain, it's good to have reference photos of what it looked like.

10 The heater has been removed and the hole is ready to be filled for an air-conditioning conversion. Parts such as these, if they work, should be kept, as you never know who might need one for a restoration project.

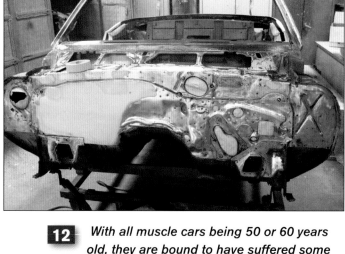

11 Interestingly, when it was being worked on some Bondo was discovered above the hole. That might be a sign of problems ahead as there was also lots of Bondo in the hood. Take photos of things like this and use them when consulting with body shops and specialists.

12 With all muscle cars being 50 or 60 years old, they are bound to have suffered some damage over the years. Of course, some will have been well repaired and others not so well. As you dig into your project, you will no doubt uncover some unexpected Bondo in the most unlikely places. Just look at the firewall in this Camaro convertible. It looks like somebody hit it with a 12-gauge and then a hammer. Nevertheless, it's only metal and it can be repaired as shown.

13 This shot of the finished engine bay, while not restored to stock specifications, shows how beautiful the Camaro firewall became after a lot of work.

14 *Keep track of all details, such as how many shims were in the hood hinge. No doubt the car will assemble differently but it's a good idea to have a starting point.*

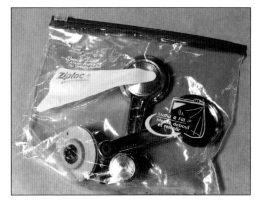

15 *Buy yourself a few boxes of sealable (Ziploc) plastic bags (you can even buy biodegradable ones now) that have spaces for labels. Put associated parts and their nuts and bolts in separate bags; for example, put all the left hand door trim in one bag and all right hand door trim in another.*

16 *You can even use bags for large parts. Just put the bag over one part and tape it on. This alone could save you weeks of hunting down the lost parts that are no longer available. Not to mention the cost of relocating lost parts.*

17 *It might even be worth it or necessary to buy a parts car, as in the case of this 1957 Ford Ranch Wagon. The car provided numerous missing parts for the actual project. Afterward, you can sell what's left.*

To Strip or Not to Strip?

As a matter of course, everything in Mick's Paint is stripped to bare metal; it's just basic common sense. Yes, it takes longer, and costs more, but he knows what he'll finish with and he shouldn't have any surprises or "come backs."

If you decide not to strip, be warned that the worst-case scenario is that you tear the car down, do your repairs, sand and prep the original paint, mask it all off, purchase the very expensive paint materials, and paint it only to discover the new paints react with the old and it all wrinkles up. That's weeks of work

and money wasted and you now have to strip it all off and start over. You might as well have done it right in the first place. And, you now have to buy another batch of expensive materials. Any enjoyment you were having from this rewarding process is well behind you now and it has cost you more than twice what it should have cost.

Wet Sand the Original Paint

et's start at the simple end of things. You want a nice paint job on a vehicle that you can't or don't want to strip to bare metal. Your only option is to wet sand it by hand and hope that whatever paint is already there proves to be a good base for a new coat of paint. For a more detailed look at color sanding, see chapter 11. ■

Whenever you are folding sandpaper to tear it, especially coarse paper, always fold with the rough side inside to save your fingers.

Despite the obvious dent, this hood (and in fact the whole car) had good enough original paint that you could wet sand it, make the necessary repairs, and paint over the top.

You should always use a good quality sanding block, the longer the blocks the better. Using your fingers will leave grooves in the surface.

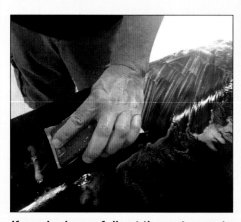

If you look carefully at the water spots behind Mick's hand, you will see that he is sanding diagonally. After sanding one way, he cross cuts the other way.

You can dry the surface of the sanded area using a 3M squeegee or by dragging the side of the rubber block across the surface to remove the water.

After you have sanded diagonally in both directions, wipe off the water and dry the surface to spot any obvious imperfections. Then you can continue until the surface is flat.

There are several ways to go about stripping your car. Your decision will be determined by your budget, the facilities you have access to, the amount of work you want to do, and the level of finish you desire: concours, show car, daily driver, or whatever.

Top Job

If your goal is a top-notch, worry-free finish then you need to completely strip the car. Mick's Paint prefers to hand strip or acid dip every project down to bare metal. Mick prefers to use W.M. Barr's Aircraft Paint Remover, which is available from any good auto body paint supplier. It is effective on acrylics, lacquers, polyurethanes, baked enamels, and epoxies.

Obviously, stripper is a hazardous chemical and should be treated accordingly. I used some recently and didn't take the time to wear gloves and a year later I still have the burn mark. Be sure to wear gloves, cover-

Yes, it will take some time to get the body of your vehicle this clean but that is what it takes if you want that show-quality finish.

alls, eye protection, and a facemask when you tackle the stripping.

There are three methods to consider to strip a car. They are media blasting, acid dipping, and hand stripping. Let's take a look at each.

Media Blasting

Depending on your location, you might be able to find a soda blaster. Certainly, they are located in big met-

ropolitan areas. What we commonly call soda is actually bicarbonate of soda, more commonly called baking soda. Near Mick's Paint is Cal Blast, which uses several Arm & Hammer media products under the Armex brand for media blasting.

Armex has several blasting media that have moisture inhibitors, flow additives, and various formulations for different substrates. The main advantage to baking soda is that it is not an abrasive as are some other media. Soda is actually a crystal. Instead of grinding off coatings (as other media do), soda actually fractures when it hits the coating and pops the coating off, leaving the substrate smooth, with little to no profiling. Armex says it can actually soda blast right over glass and chrome without pitting or damaging it. Since traditional media are abrasive, they create heat while they are stripping. This heat can cause warping, costing hundreds or thousands of dollars to fix. No heat is generated with soda blasting, therefore no warping.

You can use a DA sander to sand off the paint and any Bondo you might find hiding underneath. Begin with 80-grit on the big lumps and, as they disappear, switch to 150-grit to smooth it out while removing any scratches made by the 80-grit.

Depending upon your location, soda blasting might be an option. Check the Internet for mobile services that appear to be springing up all over the country. However, try to get some recommendations and insight to the blasters' experience with valuable sheet metal. You do not really want them to experiment on your vehicle.

Cal Blast prefers to blast a disassembled car. Since you're going to have to remove the doors, hood, trunk lid, and fenders anyway to work on them properly, this is really not a wasted chore. Just be careful not to damage them when you are loading, unloading, and transporting them.

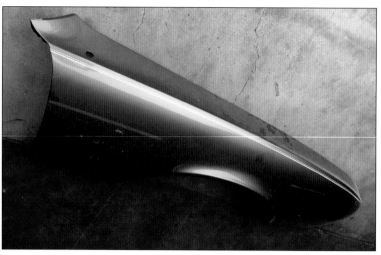

This is one of the Camaro fenders before it was soda blasted at Cal Blast. Be aware that unless you are extremely lucky, you are going to find some damage under that paint.

This after shot shows the fender completely and effectively soda blasted with no visible warpage. However, some old damage was uncovered, which is to be expected on 50- to 60-year-old vehicles. The damage revealed by the soda blasting indicates an old but thankfully small repair in the front of the fender. We hope it's not too big of a task to repair.

Various holes in the lower quarter of the front fender where there was some badging will need repairing before the job can proceed. However, it's better to find it now rather than later.

You can see that the inside of the fender that was soda blasted looks as good as the outside. After some metal prep, this is a perfect surface with which to begin your project.

Here's a close-up of the Camaro door midway through the soda blasting process. You can see that it leaves a really clean, undamaged surface. In addition, it leaves the original sound deadening that acid dipping removes.

According to Cal Blast, soda blasting will remove all old paint, rust, grease, and undercoating.

A benefit to soda blasting is that if you are not planning on a complete ground-up restoration, you can just have the exterior blasted while leaving the running gear and interior in place. That could save you a lot of time and money if you are only interested in the exterior cosmetics.

Another benefit is that some mobile soda blasters can come to you if you can't take your car to them. A quick Internet search revealed dozens. You might find one in your area.

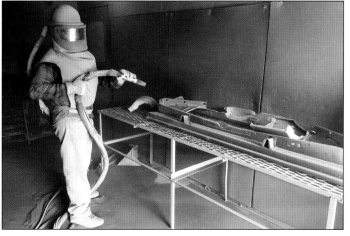
Because there is no acid dipper close to Pure Vision Design, Steve Strope uses A & M Sandblasting in Chatsworth, California, for stripping all of his muscle car builds. A & M does an incredible job using a variety of media including glass, but it primarily uses aluminum oxide.

If you're going for the full monty, that is a complete strip down to bare essentials, then the body will need to be mounted on a rotisserie in order for the underside to be blasted clean.

This truck fender was blasted at A & M using aluminum oxide. As you can see, it came out clean with no sign of damage. Beware, however, that you will need to know that the blaster knows what he's doing and that he'll be careful with your valuable sheet metal.

Dustless Blasting, based in Houston, Texas, has been around since 1941 and advocates three blasting systems: sand, soda, and water. The water is said to be around 92-percent dust-free. A rust inhibitor will, they say, prevent flash rust and ensure that the surface is clean. (Photo courtesy of Dustless Blasting)

Walnut shells are a biodegradable, nontoxic, environmentally safe, and cost-effective material for blasting. The ground shells are coarse to extra fine, depending on the application. They are durable and can be reused in many applications. Supposedly, they remove matter from surfaces without scratching or pitting underlying material. Note: Some media blasting can cause the kind of damage seen on the GTO hood.

Many companies now offer a mobile blasting service. Frank Weinert, shown here blasting a truck on location, uses soda, but other companies use other media so check before you book them. And remember, unless they use water, there will be some cleanup. (Photo Courtesy Matt Joseph)

Typically, most sand blasting is done by specialist facilities on large parts such as frames and suspension components. Small parts can be done in a blasting cabinet, but Mick does not like any sheet metal to be sand blasted as it is too easy to distort the metal. In all cases, he prefers acid dipping.

Acid Dip

Chemical stripping, or acid dipping, is a very effective way to remove paint and rust. Unlike sanding or media blasting, chemical stripping cleans the metal with solutions of caustic soda to soften and remove the paint then muriatic acid to attack the rust. We found L & M Stripping in Van Nuys, California, which specializes in this process. L & M did say that the process can take anywhere from a few days up to a week to complete. Nevertheless, it's a very effective first step to prepare metal parts or entire car bodies for bodywork because all of the metal surfaces are equally cleaned at the same time.

Metalworks in Eugene, Oregon, is another company that offers chemical stripping. Its informative website even offers prices; for example, a Mustang body shell costs only $1,850 to strip.

Strip Clean in Santa Ana, California, offers acid dipping and has a very good reputation. The beauty of Strip Clean's process is that everything is totally stripped and washed

clean so if you want to start with a totally clean sheet, this is the way to go. Another bonus is that once the parts are neutralized the process leaves a light corrosion proofing on the steel. Mick has had bodies left in bare steel while being worked on for up to a year, so this added protection is welcome.

Of course, having every inch of sheet metal stripped does create a lot more work. It now means that all of the factory seam sealer, rust proofing, and paint inside the panels will need to be replaced, but if you want it right, it's the only way to go.

Research the services that are available close to you because acid dipping is not a service you find in every town; there are only two in the whole of Los Angeles. Get references whenever possible. I've seen instances where two doors and a decklid on a genuine Boss 302 Mustang were not neutralized thoroughly and all three panels corroded where acid was trapped in the flanges and ate its way through. Typically, after acid dipping it is essential to prep the

This Mustang was delivered to Strip Clean in Santa Ana, California, and is going to be prepared for the first stage of acid dipping. To drop it whole into a tank of acid, the cost is about $1,800.

Strip Clean's acid-dipping tank is ready to take a full-size body. The entire acid-dipping process takes about ten working days.

After the acid-dipped parts are neutralized, they are dipped in another solution to protect them from rusting.

Strip Clean says that the acid-dipping process does not affect rubber components, such as these suspension bushings. However, it will remove all body sealer and rust proofing.

These 1957 Chevy truck fenders went for acid dipping to Strip Clean in Santa Ana, California. Strip Clean is one of only two shops in all of Los Angeles that offers that service.

One pro of acid dipping is that it gets to all those hard-to-reach places. A con is that it does strip out all the old sealer, sound deadening, and other things you will have to replace.

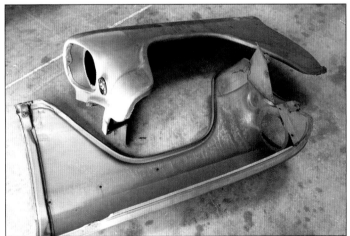

A week to ten days later, you get back two incredibly well stripped fenders. The cost in Los Angeles is approximately $200 per fender.

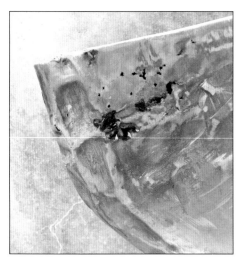

As with any stripping process, acid dipping can expose more problems than you counted on, but that's actually good. Better to find it now rather than later when it's painted.

metal before proceeding. To do that, you need to sand the panels down to bare steel with a DA sander using 150 discs then clean up the panel with a clean rag and a good degreaser.

Chemical Stripping by Hand

Chemical stripping by hand is a good but messy way to go. You can do it at home, in your own time, and for just the cost of materials. However, you do need a plan, the right equipment, and a bucket of elbow grease, as it can be hard work. Understand, this is very messy work and if you're a messy worker, it will get, well, very messy.

If you live in a damp or humid region, we recommend stripping one or two panels at a time. The reason is simple if you have seen how quickly clean bare sheet metal can begin to oxidize. It can and will visibly begin to corrode the same day. If you get carried away and strip the whole car in onc day without any means to seal it, you will spend the next day removing all the new surface rust.

Begin by covering the work area floor with heavy plastic or even a tarp; this will protect a nicely finished garage floor. Some strippers can even attack plastic flooring. Next, put newspaper, cardboard, or masking paper around the perimeter of the vehicle to catch the bulk of the spillage. This layer helps to preserve the floor and can be easily removed from the plastic later.

After protecting your workspace, we suggest you unbolt any body panels that can be removed, including doors, hood, decklid, even fenders if they are bolted on. This way you can gain access to the doorjambs, flanges, etc. It's also easier to strip some of those pieces up on a bench or a workstand, and having the panels horizontal means that they stay coated and damp longer.

Mask off everywhere on the car that you don't want the paint stripper to go, as the stripper typically creeps into places you don't want it. Imagine a large glob of chemical stripper running down your dash and melting the plastic and staining or "eating" the difficult-to-replace instruments.

To avoid that, mask off the window and door apertures, scoops, holes in panels, seams between panels, and the engine bay. Mask off the big openings with cardboard and duct tape. Do not use newspaper; it will get soggy and collapse.

Obviously, before you start stripping put on some protective clothing. Coveralls, gloves, and safety glasses should always be worn when chemical stripping. You may also want to wear those hospital booties to protect your boots.

We recommend that you start by stripping the roof so that you only have to clean the lower panels once. If you start on a fender and then move up to the roof, the goop from the roof, will run down onto the fender and you will have to clean that again. Start at the top and work down. Scuff the paint on each panel all over with coarse 40-grit sandpaper, especially in tough-to-get-to edges and seams. Scratching the paint will give the stripper purchase and a head start in eating into the paint. Do not use a blade or scraper to scuff paint, as it can scratch the metal.

Chemical Stripping

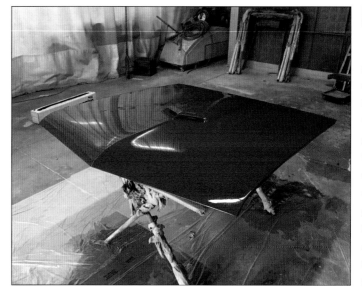

1 First, protect the workshop with plastic sheeting and paper or cardboard. The GTO hood is positioned on workstands that are wrapped in masking paper for protection. Also, the workshop floor has been protected with plastic sheeting.

Chemical Stripping *continued*

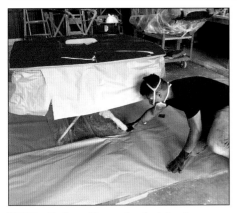

2 Before the actual stripping process, Mick protects the floor of his shop with masking paper laid on top of the plastic sheeting. You can use paper or cardboard.

3 Any trim, such as the hood scoop in the case of this GTO, should be carefully removed. Place the parts in labeled bags for future reference. The cast scoop will have to be carefully stripped or, better still, acid dipped if that is available to you.

4 Once the scoop has been removed, the hole must be masked off so as not to allow the stripping media to run into the cavity, where you will not be able to clean up the residue. A better solution is to have the hood and other removable panels acid dipped.

5 The surface of whatever panel you are stripping should be scuffed with 40-grit sandpaper to give the stripping media some purchase into the paint. Do not use a blade or a scraper for this, as it may damage the hood.

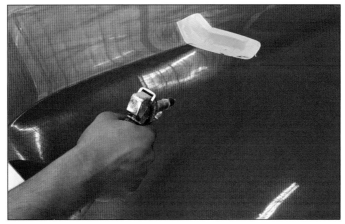

6 Once the hood has been completely scuffed with 40-grit sandpaper, the residue dust should be blown off with an airline.

7 Wear protective gloves and a facemask when the stripper chemical is poured into a mixing cup. Also, the workspace should be well ventilated, preferably with a fan to extract the fumes.

8 A small paintbrush should be used to spread the stripper evenly onto the surface of the panel. The brush should be used to work the stripper into the scuff marks.

9 If you are lucky, the paint will start to bubble up within a few minutes. The fumes are strong, so be sure to wear a mask and use a fan to ventilate the workspace.

Chemical Stripping *continued*

10 Wear gloves at all times when working with stripper. Keep a bucket of water handy to rinse away the inevitable splash of stripper because it burns.

11 The stripper soon begins to work its magic. When you see the majority of the paint bubble up like this, you can get ready to scrape.

12 Mick uses a homemade scraper that accepts a regular razor blade to attack the surface paint. However, care must be taken not to gouge the metal, as that will mean more work. The technique is to push under the paint and not dig into it.

13 As you can see the razor blade easily lifts the topcoat, but the primer is not affected. Another coat or two of stripper will be necessary to soften the substrates.

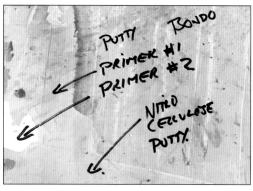

14 As you can see here, the removal of the topcoat has revealed two different primers, some body putty, and some Bondo. Unfortunately, it has also revealed some nitro cellulose putty, which is not good because it shrinks badly and, since it has no activator, it takes forever to dry.

15 Another coat of stripper will be necessary to remove each layer of primer and Bondo. In fact, it eventually took five applications of stripper to get all the Bondo.

16 To increase the chemical action of the stripper, plastic sheeting can be laid over the wet stripper and left overnight. This will allow the stripper to get into the substrate materials without drying out.

17 By the next morning, the stripper has done its job. The Bondo now scrapes up fairly easily; however, six patches of fairly deep filler were uncovered. This was not a good sign.

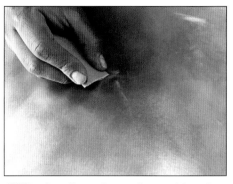

20 *Any lingering paint residue that the DA cannot reach (because it's in a hole) can be removed by hand with sandpaper.*

19 *The filler and what's left of the primer and paint should be removed with a DA sander and 80-grit sandpaper. Remember to keep the sander flat and to use a mask to prevent dust inhalation.*

18 *With as much of the paint as possible removed with a scraper, the surface was then neutralized with lacquer thinner. The remaining residue was removed with a DA sander and 80-grit paper. Do not use coarser paper and do not use a grinder to remove residue.*

21 *Those six sinkholes aligned with the voids in the hood frame and were so deep that the hood would eventually be scrapped. They were caused by excessive heat/pressure from previous sand blasting. I hope that you won't experience that sinking feeling.*

Stripping Fiberglass

Not too many muscle cars were made entirely of fiberglass, thankfully. Only the Corvette was completely fiberglass; however, over the years a lot of muscle cars, especially those that have been raced, have been fitted with fiberglass hoods, fenders, bumpers, and maybe even doors. Of course, many of those cars from the late 1960s into the 1970s had Endura or some other kind of plastic appendage. If you're stripping such a car then exercise even more care so as not to damage the parts during the process. Mick's Paint prefers to scrape the paint off the fiberglass with a razor blade instead of using a chemical stripper.

Yes, that sounds crazy and excessive, but in Mick's opinion it's the only way to go as it inevitably saves time, trouble, and certainly cleanup. You can tell Mick doesn't like using stripper. If you prefer to use a chemical, Klean Strip Aircraft Paint Remover will work or Klean Strip has a chemical specifically designed for fiberglass. It's a little cheaper than the regular Aircraft stripper at around $33 a gallon.

If you go the stripper route, follow the instructions in the preceding section. Proceed carefully, strip one area at a time, and watch the reaction of the base. Very few of those 1950s and 1960s cars have survived completely unscathed; they have all been damaged at some time to some extent and you don't want to find the stripper eating more than you anticipated.

As it was, Randy Ricklefs, son of renowned pinstriper Dennis Ricklefs, didn't have too much trouble stripping a 1962 Corvette on behalf of Wheeler Speed Shop in Huntington Beach, California. He used a razor blade to remove the red paint and then the yellow primer. The work is tedious and time-consuming, but not difficult and the cleanup is minimal.

This 1962 Corvette was in for a complete repaint, but first it had to have its trim removed, bagged, and labeled. Note the LS conversion.

It doesn't seem possible but razor blades were used to strip the red paint and yellow primer from this 1962 Corvette. It's difficult work but better than a messy strip job in Mick's opinion.

It takes time and patience to strip with a razor blade. While you have to be careful not to dig into the body and cause more damage, the benefit is that you can worry less about the stripper getting into places where you don't want it.

Yes, there is some cleanup when stripping with a razor blade, but it is nowhere near as much as there would have been with stripper. An added benefit is the cost is a lot less in terms of chemicals and materials.

Of course, there were the inevitable repairs to be made. The majority of 1950s and 1960s cars have been damaged at some time in their lives.

With all the paint removed and no mess, you can see what you're getting into. Obviously there's the usual damage and cracking around the grille area, but thankfully there is no substantial crash damage.

After being painted and assembled, this 1962 Corvette for Wheeler Speed Shop in Huntington Beach, California, looks stunning with better-than-factory fit and finish.

Metal Preparation

Don't skip this section because it sounds boring and you want to get to the fun stuff. As usual, cutting corners here will cost you dearly in the long run. Depending on your schedule, budget, and the amount of extra work you've now uncovered, there are several ways you can go about preparing the metal.

Before you start, consider where you live, as that can make a decision for you. If you live in a warm or a hot and dry region, you may be able to leave your car unprotected for a long time. If you live in an area with a damp or changeable climate or you are by the ocean, you will need to seal the bare sheet metal to stop surface corrosion from setting in before you start painting.

You'll need to research what brands and types of materials are available to you; some of Mick's Paint's preferred products may not be available or even legal where you live. A word of warning, some serious studying is required here. Some products, including some so-called "etch" primers, are not recommended to be applied over blasted surfaces. Who'd have thought it? Logically, that would be the way to go. Again, picture your beautiful paint job coming unglued and peeling off in sheets. Trust me, it can and does happen.

Choose your brand and check out what you think you need. Definitely get some pointers from your chosen paint store, get the manufacturer's data sheets, and don't be shy, call the manufacturer with questions or get the paint store to do it for you. If they are not keen to assist you, move on. You are going to be spending some serious money with them, don't accept comments such as, "That should work," or, "I think so." You need to know for certain that you are using the correct prep materials.

Once you have the materials that you need, it is time to plan your attack. Typically, Mick's Paint seals everything inside and out before beginning any assembly of sheet metal for alignment setup. That sounds simple, right? Wrong.

If the surfaces to be sealed and/or etch primered aren't prepared meticulously, you'll be watching expensive paint fall off later. Check what the paint manufacturer calls for in the way of prep before applying the material. NOTE: They will assume that you already know the basic stuff because their tech sheets are aimed at professionals. You're an amateur; you're going to need additional help and advice.

Here's what you need to do in layman's terms: Whichever method of stripping you choose, you will need clean, dry air to clean off the surfaces and eventually to push the paint through your paint gun. Oil and water in your air tank, air lines, or paint gun will kill your handiwork. So before you start, make sure you have a completely dry system. You can't have too many water traps, filters, and more filters.

If you had your project media blasted, you can and will spend hours chasing abrasives around the inside of the body and panels. The stuff is going to come out of places it shouldn't, but keep going because it will keep coming out. If you don't get it out now, it will certainly come out when you apply the topcoat color, I absolutely guarantee it.

Metal Preparation

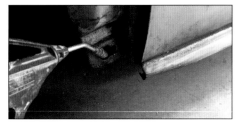

1 After the stripping process, get yourself some safety glasses, a powerful vacuum cleaner, a good source of compressed air, and a long-reach blowgun. You could easily spend an entire day cleaning out the blasting residue and still not get it all. We can't stress enough the need to be thorough at this stage.

4 A red 3M Scotch-Brite pad can be used to apply the DX579. Work a small area of about one square foot at a time and remember to change out the pad regularly as it picks up the dirt and moves it around.

7 After the surfaces have been thoroughly cleaned, all the bare metal should be re-sanded with a DA and 150-grit to ready it for a coat of PPG DP90LV epoxy primer sealer.

2 After blasting, the bare metal must be prepped. Mick prefers PPG DX579 metal cleaner for stripped steel surfaces; however, it's important to follow the manufacturer's instructions as etch primers and body filler should not be applied directly over some treatment products. For aluminum, Mick uses Turco Alumiprep 33 (now known as Bonderite C-IC 33 Aero) a nonflammable phosphoric acid–based cleaner, brightener, and pre-paint conditioner. Again, the manufacturer's instructions must be followed carefully.

5 After the metal has been prepped with the DX579, it needs to be neutralized and cleaned with acetone or even water if that's what the tech sheet calls for.

8 You will most likely find some areas that are not easily sanded, such as this rusty area on the hood.

3 A small amount of the PPG DX579 is poured into a mixing cup for ease of use. Be sure to wear gloves, glasses, and a mask in a well-ventilated area when performing this operation.

6 You will be surprised at the amount of dirt left on the surface. You will probably have to wipe it down two or three times, maybe more, to get it really clean.

9 For areas that you can't easily sand, such as drip rails or heavily pitted areas, you might want to clean them with a small sand blaster such as this handheld gravity-fed gun that Mick's Paint uses from Central Pneumatic/Harbor Freight.

PANEL DEBATE

Once you have all the paint off, you will be able to see just how much trouble you are in. Repairing body panels and parts can be a daunting task that can result in more work than you started with. Tackling this part of your project is dependent on two things: your talents and/or appetite for trying new things and your pocketbook. It can be such a mess that you have to throw down your tools and get professional help; however, I firmly believe that given patience, care, and some sage advice you can do it. You just have to tread carefully and take it piece by piece slowly.

Let's suppose that you stripped the paint off those front fenders and what you found underneath was horrifying prior repairs. You have a couple choices: Clean it up and Bondo over it or replace the panel. Replacing the panel is preferable if panels are available. However, be aware that replacement panels don't always fit as they should and that buying a panel does not mean your work is done. It's not.

Let's take a look at a few examples and see what the professionals decided to do.

1971 GTO Convertible Quarter Panels

As I just mentioned, you might find a horrific repair. Take a look at the accompanying images of a 1971 Pontiac GTO convertible and you will see the revelation of some horrifying repairs. If this happens to you, your only recourse is to soldier on, knowing that when you're done the structure of your project will be as good as you can make it.

There were some gnarly repairs to the GTO. Check out where the top and lower parts of the rear fender were joined and brazed together. This was not a great foundation for a restoration project.

They only made 678 convertible Pontiac GTOs in 1971, so the owner thought he had gone to heaven when this one was found. Unfortunately, once the paint was removed some body rot was found along with some previous repairs that were less than perfect. Nevertheless, all of it is fixable; it just takes time and materials.

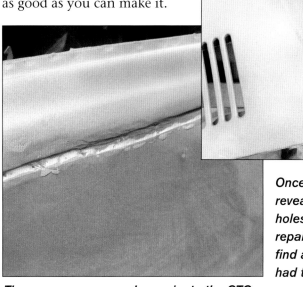

Once stripped, the hood revealed dozens of tiny rust holes that were really beyond repair. The only answer was to find another hood. In the end, it had to be fiberglass.

Only coupe quarter panels were available for the 1971 Pontiac GTO, and so coupe fenders were purchased from Dynacorn. They were cut and spliced into the original convertible quarter panel tops.

Here, Poncho uses an air-powered cut-off wheel in a die grinder to cut away the old, rotted out lower part of the quarter panel. He's cutting to the line edged with tape. Notice the body clamps holding the quarter panel top in place.

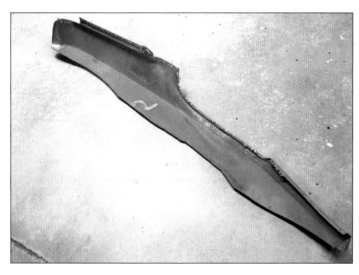

This is the only salvageable part from the top of the convertible GTO's rear quarter. The bad part was removed using an air-powered cut-off wheel. The good section will be refitted to the car.

As you can see, the cut-off wheel makes for a very clean cut. Great care has to be taken while grinding, as the new lower panel needs to butt up against that perfectly. Note: This is the other quarter.

Here you can see the inside of the rear fender after Poncho has welded the new bottom to the old top. Obviously, great care has to be taken not to warp the panel.

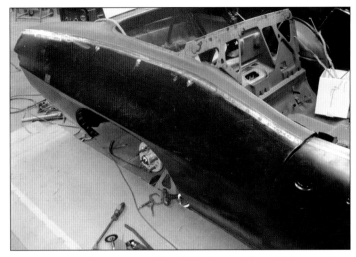

You can see the very precise fit between the old top and the new bottom here. The fit needs to be perfect before the seam is tacked every inch or two prior to welding.

After the seam has been completely welded, the joint is ground down to a smooth finish. But you must take care not to grind through the welds.

You'd never know, and you shouldn't, that most of this rear fender from the top down has been replaced. Here it has been coated with PPG DP90 epoxy sealer.

Something you must do as you go along with the repair is make sure that parts that bolt on, such as the convertible top trim or the taillight, fit properly.

1971 GTO Convertible Front Fenders

The front fenders of this 1971 Pontiac GTO convertible were not much better than the rear quarters. They had been badly repaired; new lower quarters were just lapped over the old panels and Bondo was applied. It was a mess, and the only way to move forward on a car of this caliber was to cut away all of the previous repair and graft on new sheet metal from Dynacorn.

A NOS front fender was located for the GTO because the ones on the car were shot. However, the only fender available was for a LeMans that had the holes for the side marker lights in the wrong location.

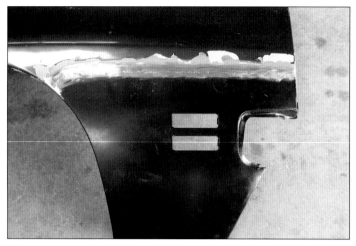

The same method of repair that was used on the rears was also used on the front fenders. The rusty lower areas were cut away using a cut-off wheel and the new panels were carefully cut to fit and welded in place.

When looking up inside the front fender, you can see where the new lower part was welded to the original upper part of the fender.

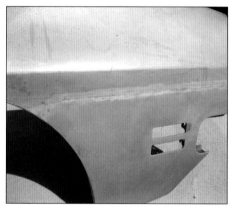

The finished fender looks as good as new. After the repairs, the paint was stripped by hand before the fender was washed and metal prepped.

This close-up shows the front fender after it was repaired, cleaned, and coated with metal prep. As you can see, it is a combination of original parts and NOS parts. Sometimes it's the only answer.

For metal prepping steel, Mick's Paint prefers to use PPG DX579. It is a multipurpose phosphoric acid–based cleaner and pre-paint conditioner to deep clean a metal surface prior to painting.

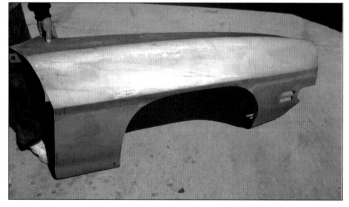

The completely finished front fender was cleaned and metal prepped. It is now ready to be painted with PPG DP90LV epoxy primer sealer.

After all of the body repairs were complete, the GTO was shot in black PPG DP90LV epoxy sealer primer for protection. Final shaping can and will be performed on top of this sealer.

Misaligned Panels

Anyone who is remotely familiar with cars of the 1950s, 1960s, and 1970s will know that in most cases the factory panel fit and alignment was abysmal. If you got a so-called "Friday" car, you were lucky if there were any bolts holding the fenders on. The cars were just not that well engineered or assembled and the public seemed to accept this.

Eventually, Japanese and German automakers began to address fit and finish. You may remember the old Lexus ES television ad from 1992 where they had a ball bearing running along the gaps between body panels to show how consistent they were. The ad claimed, "We've achieved extremely tight tolerance between all body panels." It was a game changer. Even if the factories were slow to pick up on the concept, hot rodders and custom car builders such as Lil' John Buttera and Boyd Coddington accepted the challenge and applied the "tight gap" philosophy to their early Ford hot rods and custom cars such as *CadZZilla* and *CheZoom*.

Since then, if a car didn't have consistent gaps from the factory, restorers and custom builders have been chasing the gap, trying to make them narrow and consistent to extremes. If you're restoring for judging, then it's worth contacting the judging group for your particular make and model and see what its guidelines are. If you're building a show car, then the gaps need to be consistent.

Perfectly fitting the panels is not something that you do at the end of the project. You do it at the metal-shaping stage when you make sure everything fits, shuts, and opens

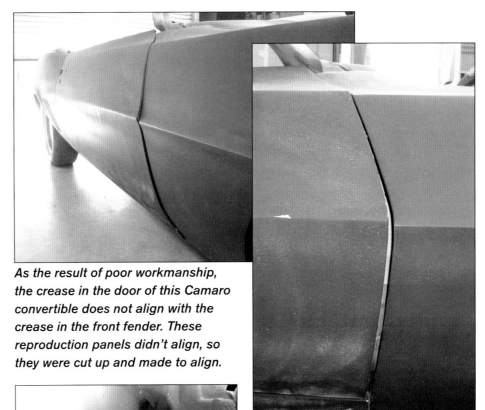

As the result of poor workmanship, the crease in the door of this Camaro convertible does not align with the crease in the front fender. These reproduction panels didn't align, so they were cut up and made to align.

From the side it looks worse. You can see how the door gap widens as it gets lower and that the swage line in the door does not align with the fender.

The same fender looks low in comparison to the door top. Some less-than-satisfactory repair work has been performed here.

Removal of the paint and an abundance of Bondo revealed a very scary but typical poor repair. Note: This is the same door shown above.

as it should. Panels need to be fit with metal not Bondo, as you wouldn't want to catch an edge and have it fall out.

One thing to remember is that if you do all the metal work on the frame and then remove the body for painting, you might find that it bolts down differently when assembling the body back on the frame and now the doors don't fit the way they did before. All you can do is make sure you have the same blocks and/or shims in the same place and that

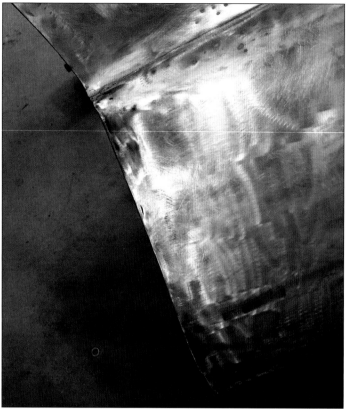

Once stripped, it was easy to see that the trailing edge of the front fender, while not as bad as the door, showed some shoddy repairs. It was better to get a new fender.

A project can be very daunting when it's down to a bare frame and all you can see ahead of you is lots of work. Keep reminding yourself that it's worth the effort.

Metal was added to the trailing edge of the front fender. It could then be trimmed so that the gap was parallel and consistent.

Panel alignment is critical if you're building a show-quality car; a great deal of time and patience goes into getting it right.

The result is probably better than factory because these three panels never aligned this well when the Camaro rolled off the production line.

After a great deal of restoration work at Pure Vision Design and Mick's Paint, the 1969 Camaro 350 SS convertible looked better than new, certainly in the fit and finish departments.

One unforeseen problem with the Camaro came with the aftermarket decal kit that did not fit at all. Eventually, Dennis Ricklefs had to do it all by hand.

you cinch all the body bolts while carefully checking that the doors open and close as they did. This can be a tedious, time-consuming process that takes more than one person to accomplish, but it has to be done and done right.

When you're searching for your ideal car to restore, you're going to see lots of misalignment and it's something to beware of. Ignore the seller who says that it just needs a bit of adjustment. That bit of adjustment just might not be possible without of lot of work.

GTO Convertible Alignment

1 Unfortunately, some time elapsed after the GTO convertible had been put into primer before it was possible to get back to work on it. It had to go back to Pure Vision Design for a chassis alteration, where, unfortunately, all of the front sheet metal had been removed.

GTO Convertible Alignment *continued*

2 Here, Poncho is adjusting the door before installing the fender to be followed by the grille, headlights, and bumper.

3 With the exception of the left-hand headlamp bezel, most of the front end is back in place. Note that all of these parts are now fiberglass because it is possible to manipulate the glass but not so the plastic Endura bumper.

4 It takes a lot of time and effort to adjust these original and non-original parts so that the gaps are consistent; something they never were from the factory.

5 After all of the front end has been assembled, Paco works on the rear fenders, making sure that the body lines are sharp, consistent, and, above all, straight.

6 Paco uses a light to check his work and make sure that the highlights he's carefully sanding are straight and perfect.

7 *It's delicate work getting the curvature of the slight fender flare correct between the lip and the body crease. You can see here how Paco tweaks his block to achieve the right contour.*

8 *Still a lot of block sanding has to be done before the GTO is ready for paint, but it's getting there. You can see how straight that horizontal crease that runs through the middle of the car is going to be.*

Lead or Bondo Panel Repair?

In Mick Jenkins's opinion it's not a matter of a choice between lead and Bondo; he would never choose lead. In fact, whenever a car comes into his shop he is meticulous about removing any and all lead and replacing it with modern filler.

"Lead is what the manufacturers used in the early days for joints and seams, and it's what the early customizers used when they were creating this industry," said Mick. "They didn't have Bondo and they certainly didn't have the advanced materials that are available to us today. Back then there was no choice. Today, we have choices and I would never use or recommend lead."

The other reason Mick abhors lead is because it can contain contaminants. The flux used to make the lead adhere to the metal and the materials used to lubricate the paddle that is used to position the lead

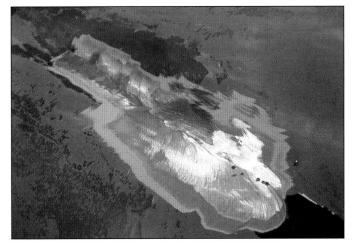

Here's an example of why Mick Jenkins doesn't like lead. Look at the string of pinholes that have been caused by contaminants in the material that eventually bubbled up through the paint.

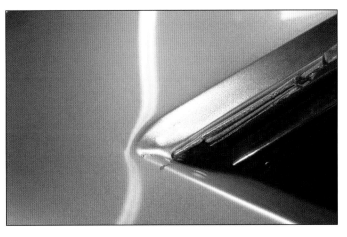

This car came into Mick's Paint because the owner had seen some minor cracking in the paint around the window at the fender-to-roof seam. It didn't look like much, how bad could it be?

are acidic and they sweat and push their way up through the paint. Lead also expands and contracts, causing the paint to crack, not to mention the cost, labor, tools, and skill required to apply the material. There are very few people who can apply it correctly and even the best cannot guarantee a long-term result. In Mick's opinion, it's just not something you should ever consider.

That said, we have seen lead applied at Mick's Paint, but it was purely for a magazine photo shoot and a display where they wanted the car to look as if it was finished in bare metal. To create that look, lead was used as filler; however, as soon as the shoot and the show were over, the lead was removed.

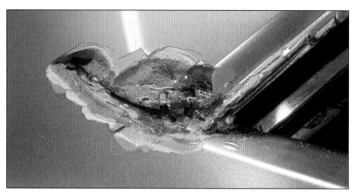

Some judicious digging revealed some thick Bondo with worse below, as there was some rust around a badly leaded seam.

Further digging and grinding exposed the fact that it was much worse than initially expected, proving Mick's iceberg theory that if you can see the tip what's below the surface is much worse.

The only time Mick will allow lead to be used is when a car has to be photographed or displayed in bare metal, then and only then is lead acceptable. This is the rear fender of Bob Florine's 1957 Ford Del Rio Ranch Wagon prior to filling for the photo shoot.

Lead is being applied by heating the material with a torch and allowing the lead to build up on the body. The flux allows the lead to adhere to the metal. The tallow is used to lubricate the paddle that is used to push the lead around.

All smoothed out and looking cool for photo shoots and displays. In Mick's opinion that is the only thing lead is good for. After the photo shoot, the lead was completely removed.

A body file was used to rough the lead into shape and then 80-grit sandpaper was used to get a smooth finish. Metal shaper Joey Angelo handled the lead work as well as a lot of the metal shaping on the wagon.

Look at the rear fenders and hood on Billy F Gibbons's CadZZilla that Mick had to repaint because the contaminants in the lead were pushing up through the paint.

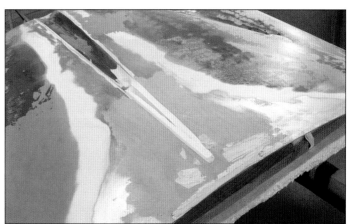

There was so much going on under the paint in terms of lead contamination that in the end it was decided it would be far better to strip and repaint the entire car.

Bob Florine's 1957 Ford Del Rio Ranch Wagon was displayed at the 2017 Grand National Roadster Show in bare metal, lead and all.

What Is Bondo?

Due to metal shortages during and after World War II, automotive panels became thinner and larger, with a greater susceptibility to warping. An alternative to lead came with the invention of plastic solder around 1940. These one-part epoxy-based fillers gave the consumer a do-it-yourself solution. In 1955, veteran and automotive repair shop owner Robert Merton Spink of Miami, Florida, invented what we know today as Bondo. It was a two-part mix of talc and plastic that had a hardener added.

There are some specialty fillers available today that contain metal, such as USC all-metal that contains aluminum and can be used where extra strength is needed. However, some of these fillers have an activator that does not cause a color change when mixed, making it extremely difficult to know when the two parts are fully combined. Amateurs should be careful using these products and make certain they are mixed properly.

Today, there are many filler materials on the market. If this is your first go around, maybe get some advice from your local body shop or just get an old panel and fill some dents. It's always worth experimenting, as some don't work over bare metal and some just don't perform well, even though they might be expensive.

Bondo and How to Apply

At Mick's Paint there are two scenarios for Bondo:

1. Over bare metal that has been properly prepared.
2. Over DP primer sealer that has been allowed to dry thoroughly and then sanded.

In both situations, Mick highly recommends that you always refer to the manufacturer's data sheets for clear guidance and that you always prepare the surface well and not cut corners.

Mick said, "In the past it was common to see body men rough out the surface and then 'finish' it with a body file or a grinder and 40-grit. It was fast and easy and the rough surface helped hide any imperfections. Today, that's just not acceptable because the Bondo can shrink back into those deep grooves and cause problems later on.

"In my opinion, the surface on which the Bondo is to be applied should be such that it will not allow the Bondo to shrink. Good prep work is good insurance against problems that might surface later. I never put more Bondo over 40-grit scratches, I always go over the 40- with 80-grit paper and then add more Bondo if necessary. As always, perfection is in the prep."

Applying Bondo

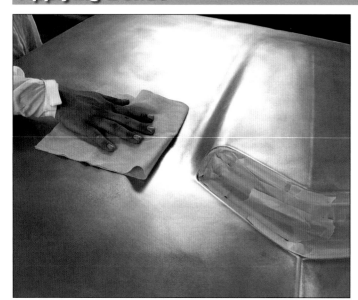

1 In the case of bare metal, Mick will sand it using a DA and 150-grit. He works one panel at a time because the bare metal oxidizes. After sanding the metal, he cleans it with degreaser (shown) and then applies the Bondo.

2 If the area requiring Bondo has been coated in DP primer sealer, as was the inside of this hood, Mick likes to rough it up with 150-grit; however, if it's an area that requires a delicate touch, such as drip rails, corners, the edges of doors, he'll use red Scotch-Brite.

Applying Bondo *continued*

4 Bondo should be used sparingly, but in some cases you just have to use a sufficient amount to achieve the required shape. Spread it carefully using a plastic spreader.

3 Mixing the Bondo and the hardener consistently is extremely important; too much activator or activator that is not mixed thoroughly can bleed through the paint. If you are working in a cold environment, you can gently warm the panel to be worked.

5 Don't scrimp. Always mix enough Bondo to float the area in one go. Do not mix a small amount to fill a large indentation. And go far out so that you have enough material to feather the edges.

6 If you are impatient you might be tempted to knock the Bondo back with 40-grit and then fill it with primer surface. However, those big grooves can give the subsequent coats somewhere to sink into. Use 40-grit to knock the surface off but clean up the scratches with 80- and then 150-grit.

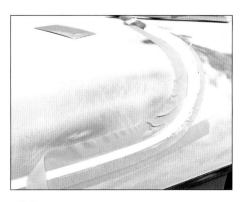

7 Don't sand the Bondo too early; allow it to dry properly before you attack it. If you sand too early it could peel off at the edges and will clog the sandpaper, which should be kept clean with a blowgun. Wherever possible, sand diagonally in opposite directions.

8 Always use some kind of block to support the sandpaper. If you're using a long block, be sure to space your hands for even pressure.

9 If you have defined lines be sure to tape the edges and block sand to those lines, ensuring that the lines remain consistent and straight and retain their edges.

Applying Bondo *continued*

10 According to Mick, 80 percent of shaping is done with 80-grit. You want to see sharp and well-accentuated body lines, such as the ones on the roof of the wagon.

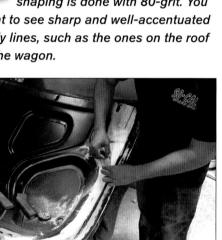

11 Even on the underside of the hood you can see that Poncho uses a variety of blocks and techniques to get the surfaces where he wants them.

12 Some might think filling and sanding the underside of the hood is going too far but when you're building a car to be shown, this is the extent that it has to be detailed.

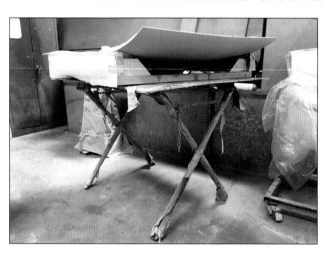

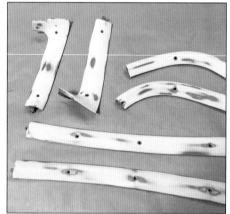

15 Specialty fillers such as USC all-metal contain aluminum and can be used where extra strength is needed. Be careful when mixing, as not all change color when the hardener is added and are therefore difficult to read. Mick does not recommend these materials for beginners.

14 Even the trim pieces need a little bit of filler to make them perfect. This shot gives you some idea of the amount of work it takes to complete a show finish.

13 When large panels are being worked on off of the vehicle, such as the hood shown here, they should be well supported on a wooden form on workstands or a table.

PAINT PRODUCTS

Obviously, there are numerous paint products on the market. Some of the more common brands include Axalta (formerly DuPont), BASF, PPG, Sherwin-Williams, Spies Hecker that is actually a division of Axalta, and Valspar.

There are also companies that specialize in custom paints such as Auto Air Colors, House of Color that is a division of Valspar, Metal-flake Corp., and Paint With Pearl. Each of these companies, and others that you can find on the Internet, is worth investigating if you're looking for something different.

Through the years, Mick has pretty much tried them all and has settled on PPG products. It's not to say that the other brands are not as good, it's just that he prefers the PPG system and more or less sticks to it.

The beauty of today's world of paint is the Internet. You can visit ppgrefinish.com and delve deep into its site that offers everything from digital color matching to online training and safety. For Joe Average, there's almost too much information, but be assured if you need it it's there, somewhere. Indeed, PPG's global color database has more than 2 million formulas that can be

Mick begins the paint process with two coats of PPG DP90LV black epoxy primer to provide a good working base. It is thinned with D8774 and hardened with DP401LV epoxy hardener.

The epoxy primer is followed by PCL High Performance Hi-Fill Polyester Primer Surfacer typically beginning with two coats of black followed by four to six coats of gray. Note: This primer is very porous and should never be wet sanded or used in damp climates.

quickly accessed by its paint manager software program. With customizable search options, the paint technician can quickly locate the latest color variant all in one system. This includes exterior, bumper, accent, and underhood colors.

Other large manufacturers will have something similar to PPG, so whatever brand you decide upon you can go to its website and learn more than you ever thought you could know about paint. Incidentally, modern automotive paint is a sophisticated

Between the PCL polyester primer surfacer and the color coat, Mick applies a light coat of PPG DP90LV, DP50LV, or DP40LV non-sanding epoxy primer to enhance adhesion. Note: DP90, 50 and 40LV are different colors and you should choose the color according to the proposed color coat. For example, you would use DP90LV that is black under a black color coat so that if you should get a road chip, it shouldn't show through. Incidentally, the DP90, 50, and 40 all use the same DP401LV epoxy hardener.

For the underside of the car, Mick prefers Smart Bed Liner that is oversprayed with body color and satin clear coat.

blend of resins, binders, fillers, additives, and carrying agents (either solvents or, more commonly these days, water).

If you're a newbie, then you're going to need a lot of advice, direction, and help from your local paint store. For all practical purposes that means to do more or less as Mick does and stick to one brand of paint that has been engineered for compatibility across the range from primers through to clear coat. There's less chance that way for any weird reactions. In Mick's opinion, it's imperative that you study the manufacturer's data sheets, something you can do on their websites, before

you ever buy a tin of paint. There are rules, regulations, and best practices that should be adhered to.

Mick's only deviation to his plan is the use of PCL High Performance Hi-Fill Polyester Primer Surfacer. PCL is a manufacturer of compliant automotive refinishing products that is located in California. Through experience, Mick knows that it is compatible with the other products he uses. That said, be careful of mixing and matching.

The actual paint used on the project featured in this book was PPG Envirobase EHP that they say is the most technically advanced waterborne product available. It is thinned with T494; however, these products are susceptible to humidity. It is highly recommended that you study the associated data sheets for optimum results.

After the application of color and any graphics, Mick prefers to use PPG D8188 Glamour LV Clearcoat reduced with D8774 thinner and activated with D8384 medium hardener.

Single Versus Multistage

At one time, there was only single stage paint; that is to say, paint of a single color that is applied in one stage, much like house paint. For Henry Ford, that might have been black, but by the mid-1920s General Motors was experimenting with metallic paint, albeit single stage. Fast-forward to the mid-1950s when clear coat became readily available, heralding the birth of two-stage paint; that is to say, a single stage of color and a second stage of clear. Hence, two-stage paint. Here is a brief explanation of the different stages.

Single Stage

Single stage (ss) is what the name implies in that there is only one layer of paint in which the color and the gloss are combined and applied to the car as one. Pretty much all cars, including muscle cars, were painted ss until the 1980s. Some restorers might want original ss paint and some judging groups might also demand that. It's best to check before you dive in.

Two Stage

Again, it is what the name implies, two stages with the first being a color (solid, metallic, or whatever) and the second being a protective clear coat. The abbreviation for this base coat/ clear coat system is bc/cc.

Three Stage

Three stage paint jobs have multiple layers comprising a ground coat color that could be black, white, silver, gold, etc.; a so-called color layer that could be Metalflake, candy, pearl, etc.; and a final clear coat.

Multiple Stage

Several automakers, such as Porsche with its GT Silver and Nissan with its Super Silver on the GT-R, are offering multiple stage paint and charging accordingly. Multiple stage paint consists of base coat, silver coat, clear coat, metallic coat, and another clear coat process, some of it hand rubbed. Unfortunately, although Super Silver looks good, the GT-R forums do not give the extra cost or the difficult repair process positive reviews.

Waterborne Versus Solvent-Based Automotive Paints

Like it or not, the world is changing and we are being regulated to move away from the old solvent-based paints to waterborne paints, and probably rightly so if they are better for the environment and a painter's health. In California, where Mick's Paint is located, Mick has no choice but to comply even though some of the paint does not seem as easy to apply as the government and the paint manufacturers would have us believe.

Conventional, solvent-based base coats have a volatile organic compound (VOC) solvent content of around 84 percent; the remaining 16 percent are the solids. A typical waterborne base coat is composed of about 70-percent water, 20-percent solids, and 10-percent solvent. Therefore, you can see the reduction in solvents is substantial and beneficial. Fewer solvents are good for the environment, good for paint and body shop staff, and, according to manufacturers, good for the industry as they say they offer cleaner, brighter hues and need less clear coat.

That might well be the case, but Mick has had several instances where the waterborne paint has just not laid down the way the old solvent-based paint did. However, he has no choice other than to use it. You might be more fortunate where you live in that waterborne paints may not be compulsory. You should check with your local paint store or go online to investigate local regulations.

Even though Mick began using waterborne paints almost 40 years ago in Europe, he still suggests the solvent-based paints for beginners where legal. Mick says, "Yes, the waterborne materials are the way of the future, there's no doubt about that, and yes, they can be somewhat cheaper than solvent-based materials, maybe as much as 30 to 40 percent, but for the amateur they are more difficult to master. The old solvent-based materials were more forgiving."

Although the basic materials might be cheaper, a shop doing lots of work should really have a spray gun cleaning machine and should use the water-based reducer for cleaning. The old solvent-based cleaners are not compatible with the new paints. That said, the waterborne reducers are typically only 20 percent of the cost of solvent-based reducers.

One of the problems encountered with waterborne materials by the inexperienced is the amount of drying time needed. This can make painting a car take longer and therefore be a more expensive process, especially if you are renting booth space. The drying time is dependent upon the airflow, temperature, and other booth conditions.

De-nibbing the base color can be a tricky operation if the base coat has not dried properly. If de-nibbing is necessary, the paint should be sanded with 800-grit paper carefully. As we said, it can be slow to dry and will tear easily if sanded too soon.

Likewise, de-masking can be problematic. The tape needs to be removed very carefully and only when the paint has had sufficient drying time. Removal too early, say in a two-tone situation as described in this book, can result in the paint lifting along the taped edge. Conversely, if the paint is too dry on the tape, it can crack and fall off.

Whichever system you choose, if you have a choice, we strongly recommend that you strictly comply to the manufacturer's guidelines. Now more than ever their instructions need to be followed.

The Order of Attack: The 30-Step Process for Painting Bob Florine's 1957 Ford Del Rio Ranch Wagon

Even in a book as comprehensive as this, it is very difficult to explain the entire intricate process of painting a vehicle to show standards. We thought it would be a good idea to give to you a compressed overview of the 30 steps taken to paint Bob Florine's 1957 Ford Del Rio Ranch Wagon. The paint scheme is not very complicated in terms of graphics (some jobs can get much more complicated); nevertheless, it is two-tone and therefore tricky enough to warrant this step-by-step procedural overview beginning with stripping and ending with buffing.

It goes without saying that your paint job could be a lot simpler, especially if it is your first and you have chosen a single stage, single color scheme. That's not a bad thing; you'll just have fewer steps to worry about. What you should concern yourself with is the underlying theme of cleanliness. You will notice as you read through the steps that the entire vehicle is cleaned, degreased, and wiped with a tack cloth numerous times. Pretty much every time a significant stage in the process is reached. We cannot overstate the need for cleanliness in the shop, in the booth, and in your work practices. Just imagine you do a year's worth of work to get your car ready to paint and a careless move at the end causes a big piece of dirt or a fly to fall into the paint, maybe in the middle of the roof, and all your hard work is put to waste. There's no easy way of fixing it. If it's a panel such as the hood or decklid, you might escape with rubbing that down and starting over, but if it's in the roof or a rear quarter you will have quite a task ahead.

Cleanliness aside, a plan, care, and following instructions are the order of the day. Today's paints are not the simple solutions they used to be, especially the water-based paints. The instructions need to be followed, quantities observed, and care taken. If you do as you are told, you could end up with a paint job to be proud of. I hope so.

Overview of the 30-Step Process for Show-Quality Paint

1 The first order of business is to strip the existing paint down to bare metal, including all Bondo, primer, etc. Mick prefers acid dipping but hand stripping is an option.

2 All stripped metal must be metal prepped following the prep manufacturer's instructions. Mick prefers to use PPG DX579 for steel surfaces.

Overview of the 30-Step Process for Show-Quality Paint *continued*

3 After the metal has been prepped, all of the body modifications to the metal are completed. Here, the tailfin and 1957 T-Bird handles were being installed. Due to the extent of the modifications, the body was in bare steel for an extended period; therefore, all surfaces were metal prepped, neutralized, sanded, and prepped for the application of DP90LV epoxy primer.

4 As things came together, all of the body panels including the doors and hood (not shown), front fenders, sheet metal, grille, and bumpers were fitted and aligned.

6 As they were shaped and surfaced, each panel was sealed for protection with black PPG DP90LV. You could also use white DP48LV or gray DP50LV.

5 After the completion of metal work, all of the body and panels were shaped and surfaced as required. This included doorjambs, frames, and closures.

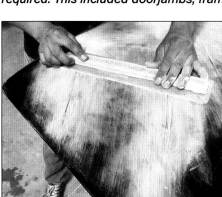

7 After sealing, each of the panels was block sanded with 150-grit to highlight any areas still requiring attention and to assure good adhesion for the primer.

8 Ideally, the day prior to the application of primer the entire car is carefully degreased with particular attention being paid to any creases or corners. Be sure to wipe or blow the degreaser dry as you go. You don't want to saturate the surface, so doing it the day before allows time for the degreaser to evaporate.

Overview of the 30-Step Process for Show-Quality Paint *continued*

9 Once the vehicle had been cleaned and degreased, it was masked prior to being wheeled back into the booth for the application of the primer.

10 Before the primer was applied, the surface was cleaned with a tack cloth. Then two coats of black PCL High Performance Hi-Fill Polyester Primer Surface No. 903 were applied.

11 After the second coat of black primer, four coats of gray PCL High Performance Hi-Fill Polyester Primer Surface No. 901 were applied. Each coat needed a 15-minute flash-off time.

12 After the primer had been allowed to dry for as long as possible, a month is good, all surfaces were block sanded dry, beginning with 150-grit and working through to 500-grit. This included blocking across adjacent panels to ensure good visual flow of highlights and shadows.

13 The vehicle was then disassembled so that all the tricky areas such as jambs, frames, and closures could be sanded for paint.

14 After the block-sanding process was complete, the vehicle was thoroughly cleaned again using PPG One Choice Degreaser.

15 Wurth seam sealer was applied to all flanges and exposed seams. The edges of the seam sealer were wiped smooth with a finger.

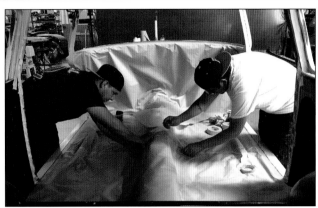

16 All surfaces not requiring paint, such as the inside and the underside of the body shell, were masked.

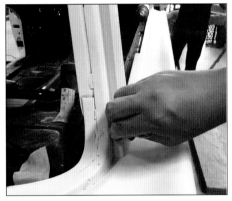

17 All exposed areas to be painted were degreased and cleaned again with particular attention being paid to difficult-to-reach places where the paint might bridge.

18 The cleaned and degreased vehicle, now ready for paint, was placed in the booth along with all necessary equipment such as benches, frames to hang parts on, gun, and filters.

19 Two light coats of DP sealer (color dependent on the color of the topcoat) were applied next. Once this had flashed off it was de-nibbed; that is to say, any minor imperfections in the surface were lightly sanded slightly wet with 800- or 1000-grit as needed and then cleaned with a tack cloth.

20 As this was a two-tone paint job, the first coat of body color was applied only to the roof; the rest of the vehicle was masked off. After color was applied, the roof was given six coats of clear coat. It would not be touched again until the color-sanding process.

Overview of the 30-Step Process for Show-Quality Paint *continued*

21 After the roof had been allowed to dry overnight, it was masked off so the second color could be applied to the bottom part of the vehicle.

22 The lighter of the two colors, the Ferrari Avorio, was applied next (excluding the roof, of course). It was followed by two coats of clear to protect the color from any subsequent damage.

23 The Avorio was allowed to dry overnight. The following day, the entire vehicle, with the exception of the roof, was sanded with 800-grit before the surfaces were thoroughly cleaned again.

24 All areas to remain Avorio were then masked using 3M Vinyl Fine Line tape to create a cleaner edge on the dividing line between the two tones. The vehicle was then cleaned again.

25 The second color, Aston Martin Bridgewater Bronze, was applied to the unmasked areas. In this case, the doors and fenders were painted separately.

26 The vehicle was carefully unmasked and all paint edges were detailed with a tack cloth to remove any errant tape, glue, or paint. Inevitably, there is some paint blow by, which is fixed at this stage.

27 Clear coat was then applied to the entire vehicle with the exception of the roof, which had been clear-coated previously.

28 The fully painted and clear-coated vehicle was allowed to dry for a minimum of a week; the longer the better.

29 After sufficient drying time, the vehicle was color sanded wet beginning with 800-grit and working gradually up through 1200-, 1500-, 2000-, 2500-, to 3000-grit.

30 Finally, when all the minute sanding scratches had been removed with the wet-sanding process, the entire vehicle was buffed to a gloss finish.

GET READY AND SQUIRT

So, you think it's that time; you think you are getting ready to paint. Stop. Wait. This is the time to go back over everything you have done so far and make certain that you are indeed ready, or almost ready, for paint.

Choose Your Color

The first question to ask yourself is what color or colors are you going to paint your car. It's always a difficult decision that is governed by a number of factors. First, what is your capability? Certainly if you have completed the prep work as outlined in this book then you have learned a lot about your capabilities and have a better understanding of both what is involved and whether you can achieve the desired results.

First timers should certainly go for the simple option of a one-color scheme, preferably in a solid rather than metallic or pearl finish. Pearls and metallics should really be reserved for the experienced painter. Do not despair; a single color using a single-stage paint might be exactly what your muscle car restoration needs. Remember, they coined some great paint names back in the

day including the Big Bad series for American Motors, Hugger Orange for the 1969 Camaro, Grabber Blue for the 1970 Boss 302 Mustang, and, my favorite, Anti-Establish Mint offered for the Mustang. Remember, a stock color might be what you need if you are intending to have your car judged for authenticity.

Choosing a single color might also be an economic decision, as it will probably be a lot cheaper than pearl or metallic and perhaps, more importantly, it will be easier to fix should you make a mistake. It will also be easier to repair and match down the road when you have had that inevitable accident.

If you've chosen to go for something more adventurous than the single-stage single color then we highly recommend that you shoot a test panel to see what the eventual color will look like. Shooting the test panel will give you an indication of how the finished car will look as well as provide some valuable practice for shooting the real thing. If you haven't got a suitable piece of metal to spray, you can always use a stainless-steel food mixing bowl to see how the color will look.

Gather All Materials

When you have chosen a color, make a list of all the paint materials you think you are going to need, everything from primer to paint and all in between. If you are inexperienced, your local paint supply store should be able to help. We have tried here to give you a guide but obviously all cars and all paint schemes are different.

Something that we can't stress enough is to buy a sufficient amount for the entire job. It's inadvisable to scrimp and buy a gallon only to run out and discover that the second gallon is a slightly different shade from the first. You need to buy enough paint plus extra because you will need some for subsequent touch ups, damage repairs, etc. Mix it all together so that you have one consistent color. (Note: Two gallons of paint will NEVER be the same and you should always mix them together for a big can of consistent color. Even if you buy three or four gallons they should always all be mixed together.)

Finally, even though paint has a reasonable shelf life if unopened, you should not let it sit for years.

Mixing Paint

When purchasing more than one gallon of paint for your project, it's imperative that you mix all the cans of paint together for a consistent color. Even formulated paints are not always the same.

Juan uses two gallon mixing buckets to mix his 2 gallons of paint. Note how he keeps the metallic particles well suspended so that they do not sink to the bottom.

When all of your cans of paint are mixed together, you should have a consistent color. Be sure to get any metallic residue out from the bottom of the can, especially if you have had the paint sitting for a while.

Refer to the date code on the can. Likewise, any catalyst (especially that has been opened) should not sit for longer than a year at most. In Mick's opinion, it's just not worth the risk of using out-of-date paint that might later cause you problems.

Preparing Your Paint Booth

Once having recapped where you are with regard to the materials you are going to use, it's time to assess the paint booth situation. I hope you are not painting your car in your back-yard and that you have access to a reasonable booth. However, do not expect to just walk in, paint, and walk away with a show-winning paint job. Nothing is that easy. The booth will need some prep work, not as much as the vehicle, but it will need to be readied for work.

With all the work they have going on, Mick's Paint's booth is fairly busy and therefore gets dusty from all the overspray. It is a constant task to keep it spic and span. In fact, the shop gets cleaned out every time it gets used and the exhaust filters are changed every time they begin a major job. The intake filters are changed annually.

The prep begins with the removal of any previously used masking paper, and then the walls and floor are swept and vacuumed. Then they wash the entire booth, walls, lights, and floor with soapy water. Before any important job, Mick has the walls sanded with a DA and 150-grit paper to remove any overspray dust that might be lingering.

After another wipe down, all of the equipment inside the booth, such as the air line filters, are masked before the walls are painted with Kilz Premium White Primer. Once that has been allowed to dry, they will completely mask the floor to prevent overspray from building up and creating dust. The air line hose is wrapped in tape again to prevent any overspray dust from coming loose and falling into the paint. Only when the booth is completely prepped is the vehicle moved in.

Something to remember, of course, is that you will have to budget for this work, the materials, and the time it will take you to prep the booth. Typically, the work outlined above will take at least three days and cost approximately $200 to $300.

Test Panels

Before you even begin to paint, it's worth shooting some test panels of your intended color scheme. If you have a spare panel from the car you intend to paint, use that; it will give you a very good idea of how the final color scheme will look. If not, any curved panel will suffice. ■

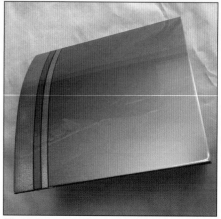

Here you can see the colors intended for Bob Florine's 1957 Ford Del Rio Ranch Wagon. The ivory is Ferrari Avorio and the root beer is Aston Martin Bridgewater Bronze. It's a stunning combination.

The blue panel was mocked up for Ed Chalupa's 1967 Ford Fairlane. Notice how the blue and gold color combination was tried along with the intended black pinstripes just to see how it would all look together.

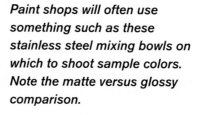

Paint shops will often use something such as these stainless steel mixing bowls on which to shoot sample colors. Note the matte versus glossy comparison.

Prep the Booth

1 *I hope that your booth was not left like this. Sometimes rented or borrowed booths are left for you to clean. Begin by removing the discarded paper and sweeping the floor and walls.*

2 *When you've removed the old masking paper and trash, sweep and then vacuum the booth well. Mick likes to wash the booth's lights as well as the walls. Wash the floor with soap and water.*

Prep the Booth *continued*

3 Before any really important paint job, Mick will have the walls of his paint booth sanded using a DA to remove the overspray dust that accumulates there.

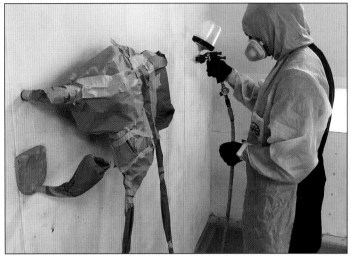

4 With everything clean, Mick likes to repaint the booth using Kilz Premium Primer Stainblocker. Note that the equipment in the booth, such as the filters, was masked to protect it from overspray.

5 Something you need to think about if you are borrowing or renting a booth is to change the filters, particularly the exhaust side, to ensure good airflow. Note: In order to even out the exhausting, filters are doubled up in the middle of the banks where the exhausting is strongest.

6 When all of the prep work is completed, mask the floor to prevent it suffering from overspray buildup and creating any dust.

7 Once the booth is clean and prepped, the vehicle can be moved in. Here, the team is wiping it down with tack rags in preparation for masking.

Prep the Booth *continued*

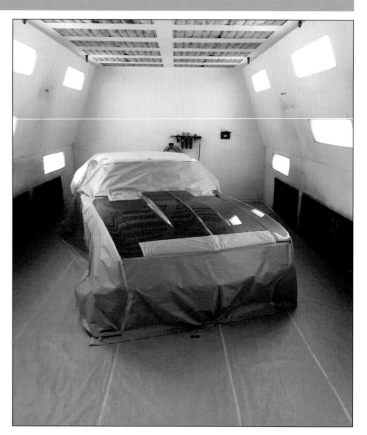

8 It's a good idea to sweep and wet down the floor outside the booth so that you don't walk in any dust as you are making preparations.

9 Here you can see that the booth is spic and span and the floor has been masked as well as the car in order to keep the dust down. Note: The car is positioned for a photo shoot; typically the car would be straight on in the booth for maximum access.

10 Mick even wraps the air line with masking tape to prevent the hose from accumulating overspray that can later be shaken loose and fall in the paint.

11 To tape the hose, hook the end to something convenient and run 2-inch tape along the length and wrap the hose.

PRIMERS AND PRIMING

In this chapter, we will go through all of the important processes that are necessary prior to paint. Following these steps will ensure the best possible surface for paint application and adhesion. Any shortcuts here will result in severe heartburn down the road.

Masking

If a job's worth doing, it's worth doing well. Be thorough and be careful. We've seen that what goes on under the primer is all-important but not more important than the primer itself. You've taken a great deal of time and trouble, not to mention money, to prepare your car properly and it makes no sense to skimp at this stage.

As mentioned in chapter 2 regarding equipment, it makes sense to purchase good rather than cheap materials. Yes, you still see painters use newspaper and whatever tape is handy to mask the car they're painting, but in Mick's world it's not acceptable. His reputation is on the line and he doesn't want any work coming back that will just cost him money and, worse, his excellent reputation.

Good quality masking paper and tape is as essential to a good finish as quality paint. Mick exclusively uses 3M Scotchblok masking paper, typically in 36-inch-wide rolls because it has a polycoated backing to prevent solvent bleed-through. It's thin enough to conform to the surfaces and yet it holds up well during wet sanding and withstands normal bake cycles. You can buy it in narrower sized 6-, 12-, and 18-inch rolls, if that's more convenient.

For masking tape, Mick prefers to use 3M Scotch 233+. It is available in a number of widths, resists solvents (something nonautomotive grade tapes do not), and as with the masking paper, can withstand 250 degrees F for 30 minutes. In the majority of instances, Mick uses the masking station to apply the tape to the paper. However, you might not have gone to that expense, so just be sure not to use the vehicle you are about to paint as a surface on which to apply the tape to the paper as it can leave glue residue that will affect your paint. Use some other clean surface to apply the tape. Most painters without a machine apply the tape to the paper on the glass of the booth door, which is

vertical, resulting in less dust. If it's dusty, wipe the glass before you tape.

Mask with as few folds and creases in the paper as possible because overspray will accumulate and dry in those creases. Later it may blow out and land in the middle of your paint or clear coat. You wouldn't want that to happen after all of your hard work.

Before you even begin to mask, think your job through and have a plan. Know which parts are going to be painted, in what color, and in what order. A plan now is only going to save you time and trouble later.

Once you have a plan but before you begin masking the large areas, go inside the body and tape off any holes there might be for trim attachment, door handles, antennas, steering column, pedals, etc. By leaving those holes unmasked you leave yourself open to dust blowing out or unwanted overspray blowing in. Neither is desirable.

Begin masking the interior. The roof, foot well, floor, and trunk space should all be masked carefully with as few creases as possible. You're always going to get a few wrinkles, but try to keep it as wrinkle free as possible. With the inside masked up, you can mask the apertures, doors, windows, etc.

Finally, mask the wheelwells as well from the bottom of the car to the floor. Why? Because you want to prevent any dust that may fall onto the floor from blowing up and into the paint. You can be as fastidious as Mick, but chances are that there will still be some errant dust floating around.

If your intention is to paint the underside of the car, you might want to consider mounting the body on a rotisserie, should you have one available.

If, for example, the roof of your vehicle is a different color from the rest of the car, as was the case with the wagon, you can mask large areas using plastic sheeting available from 3M. It can save both money and time (which equates to money). Just make sure you don't get any water between the paint and the plastic and allow it to sit, as that could cause the water to imprint in the paint. This is especially important if, for example, you paint the roof and have the lower part of the car masked with plastic while you wet sand the roof. Water is bound to seep in somewhere and it could mark the surface.

Finally, once everything is taped up and you think you are ready to paint, blow any dust off the surface and clean the entire car with degreaser. Again, you have to be careful not to oversaturate the vehicle in degreaser. Allow sufficient drying time before you paint, as the degreaser could affect paint adhesion. It is best to degrease it the day before and allow the solvents to evaporate overnight.

The following day, you can go over the entire surface with a Gerson dry tack cloth to remove any remaining dust. Mick prefers the low-tack version just to be sure no tack material contaminates the surface. Even though this has been done, sometimes Mick or one of his team will give the car another quick wipe with a tack cloth just to be sure they haven't missed anything. Now, it's time to paint.

Masking Process

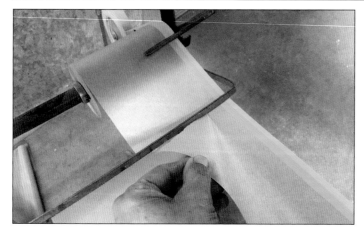

Most professional shops will have a masking station similar to this with different size paper and tape that is applied to the paper as you pull it out.

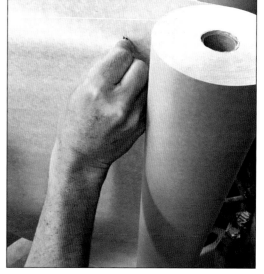

If you don't have a machine, always use a razor blade to cut the masking paper. Straight lines are so much easier to tape than jagged tears.

Masking Process *continued*

If they don't have a tape machine, most painters will apply the tape to the paper using the glass door of the paint booth. Being vertical it holds less dust, but be sure to wipe it down anyway.

You can begin by masking the many holes for trim and other items that attach through the body. This will prevent overspray from entering the body and from any dirt being blown out.

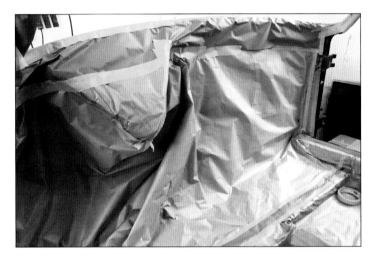

The dash and foot well are carefully masked, again to prevent unwanted overspray, dust, and unnecessary cleanup.

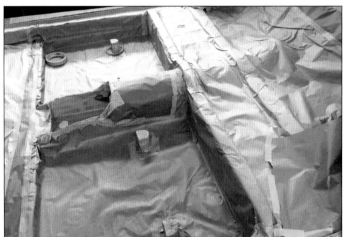

The floor pan is likewise masked to prevent any overspray. Try to keep the masking paper flat, as that will help prevent overspray getting trapped in creases and folds.

The roof is masked just like the rest of the vehicle to prevent unwanted overspray. As elsewhere, make as few creases as possible to prevent overspray buildup.

Masking Process *continued*

Finally, when the interior is masked you can mask up the apertures. Note that this masking job is not finished at the bottom.

Maybe it is not as tidy as it should be, but the wheelwells should be carefully masked, particularly around the opening to prevent overspray blowing up into the wheelwell.

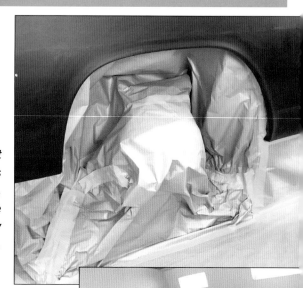

Don't forget to mask down to the floor and tape the paper or plastic to the floor. This prevents both dust blow up, should there be any, and overspray from getting into places where you don't want it.

If you're going the whole hog and painting the underside of your car, mount it on a rotisserie if possible and mask where you don't want the paint to go.

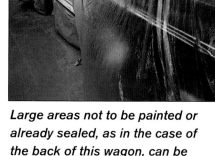

Large areas not to be painted or already sealed, as in the case of the back of this wagon, can be easily and cost-effectively masked using plastic sheeting.

THIS SIDE OUT
ESTE LADO
HACIA AFUERA

The plastic sheet might carry a "This Side Out" label. Some masking materials do have a smooth side, however, this is just there to help in unfolding the sheet.

The vehicle is now fully masked and ready for a final cleaning with a tack rag before the first coat of sealer is applied.

Sealing

After the vehicle has been degreased and allowed to dry thoroughly, preferably overnight so that all the solvents have evaporated, it is wiped down with a tack cloth to remove any dust that might have settled overnight. It is now ready for sealing; for this Mick likes to use PPG DPLV 2.1 VOC epoxy primer. These primers can be used over properly prepared steel, aluminum, fiberglass rigid plastic, and plastic fillers. They protect the surface and can be allowed to sit for days or even weeks after application. Another benefit of this material is that it cannot only be applied over body filler but body filler can be applied directly on top.

PPG's DPLV is available in three colors: white (DP48LV), gray (DP50LV), and black (DP90LV). In most cases, Mick will go with the black DP90LV as it provides a good foundation for subsequent work. The DPLV needs to be reduced with D8774 reducer and catalyzed with DP401LV hardener using the ratios provided by the manufacturer.

After the DPLV epoxy primer has been allowed to dry for at least two days (the longer the better), the vehicle is removed from the booth, unmasked, and inspected. There's bound to be a few pinholes in the surface and these can now be filled. Mick's preference is to use two-part polyester finishing and blending putty available from Evercoat's Metalworks. After any pinholes have been blown clean and filled, the surface can be worked dry using 150-grit. In addition, remember to use the longest sanding blocks you can to ensure good flat surfaces.

Applying Sealant

The day before masking, the car was thoroughly cleaned with degreaser. It's done the day before to ensure that all solvents have evaporated and are not trapped within the filler. Once the car has been masked and is ready to be sealed, it is wiped down with tack rags.

MATERIALS NEEDED

Note: All quantities are approximate and apply only to this vehicle.

3 gallons black PPG DP90LV epoxy primer

PPG DP401LV Low VOC epoxy hardener

PPG D8774 Thinner

Mixing Ratio 2 parts paint to 1 part thinner to 1 part hardener

These dry tack rags are made by Gerson and are available from any good paint supply store. They are designed for performing a final wipe over and removing any dust particles. Mick prefers the low tack version to avoid excess tack material from contaminating surfaces. If used too vigorously, traces of adhesive can be left on the surface, especially panel edges.

Applying Sealant *continued*

Even though it has been done, painter Juan prefers to make double-sure by going over the area to be sealed once again with a tack rag to pick up any errant particles of dirt.

Juan begins applying the PPG DP90LV epoxy primer sealer in the doorjambs, making sure to get good, even coverage.

After the doorjambs, Juan moves on to the other tricky areas, such as the headlights, again being careful to get good, even coverage.

After it has been allowed to dry, the sealer is dry sanded using 150-grit. Here on the hood you can see that the longest block possible is used to quickly identify any high or low spots and to ensure a flat surface. Note: The sealer can sit almost indefinitely, for days or even weeks, before being sanded.

Note how masking tape Is used to give the blocker a guide to ensure straight and consistent lines.

Any little pinholes in the sealer arc blown clean with an air gun and filled with blending putty.

Evercoat's Metalworks manufactures the two-part Metal Glaze polyester finishing and blending putty shown here with its hardener.

After sanding, the entire body is cleaned with PPG One Choice aerosol wax and grease remover.

Due to time constraints on this project, you can see here that the roof is in primer, the body is sealed and sanded, but the firewall has yet to be primed.

Priming

After the car has been sealed using PPG DPLV epoxy primer sealer, it is taken out of the booth and block sanded dry using 150-grit paper. Note: Panels can be sealed and sanded as they become ready and they are sealed to prevent contamination from moisture, sweat, dust, etc. What this effectively means is that you can work on a panel such as a door or fender, get it ready with epoxy primer, and put it aside while you work on another panel, knowing that it's not going to rust on you.

After the DPLV epoxy primer is blocked, Mick applies two coats of black PCL High Performance Hi-Fill Polyester Primer Surfacer No. 903. Each coat is allowed approximately 15 minutes drying time. The black primer is followed by four to six coats of gray PLC High Performance Hi-Fill Polyester Primer Surfacer No. 901. Again, 15 minutes drying time is allowed between coats. The reason Mick lays down black first is so that as the crew block sands the gray primer they know that when the black appears it's time to stop and not rub any further. You don't want to break through that primer; however, you can spot prime if you do, but Mick does not recommend that. It's better to stop when you see the black.

Primer

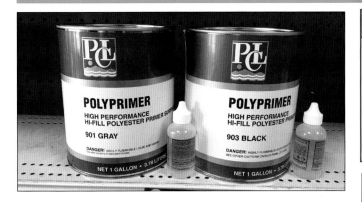

The Fairlane shown in DP90LV epoxy primer sealer is almost ready to go in the booth for priming. Note the tape used to align the body lines.

MATERIALS NEEDED

Note: All quantities are approximate and apply only to this vehicle.

2 gallons black PCL High Performance Hi-Fill Polyester Primer Surfacer No. 903

6 gallons gray PCL High Performance Hi-Fill Polyester Primer Surfacer No. 901

1.5 gallons acetone reducer

Primer *continued*

The wagon, sealed and masked and ready for primer, is now back in the booth that has also been cleaned, repainted, and masked, and is ready for work.

Because of the timetable on this project, some areas, such as the firewall, were not sealed. It doesn't matter, as they will all get primed eventually.

One gallon of black PCL High Performance Hi-Fill Polyester Primer Surfacer No. 903 is followed by 3 gallons of gray PLC High Performance Hi-Fill Polyester Primer Surfacer No. 901. Note: This is basically liquid Bondo and should not be allowed to "go off" in the gun; it is very difficult to remove, even with paint stripper.

After the black primer has been given 15 minutes to flash off, 4 to 6 coats of gray PLC High Performance Hi-Fill Polyester Primer Surfacer No. 901 are applied. Note: All primer coats are given a 15-minute flash-off time between each coat.

The first of two coats of black PCL High Performance Hi-Fill Polyester Primer Surfacer No. 903 is applied. The black will be oversprayed with 4 to 6 coats of gray primer.

Blocking

I sound like a broken record because I keep saying that each stage in this process is as important as the preceding stage, but it's true. If each stage is completed correctly before you move on to the next part then at the end you will have a paint job that is darn near perfect. Consequently, the process of dry blocking the primer prior to paint is as important as every other step. Blocking is yet another laborious, time-consuming, exacting process that requires care, and it is but one step on the road to success.

A good body man will have in his arsenal a variety of blocks that he or she uses for block sanding. Some of these blocks can be purchased from companies such as Dura-Block and, of course, from your local auto paint store. Professionals such as Mick and his team often make their own out of anything from hard foam to Lexan to wood; it all depends on the surface and the shape required.

Understanding the science of blocking is one of those things that comes with experience because what you're doing is removing scratches with each successive sanding from the initial 150-grit all the way through to the 500. It takes a certain skill to be able to see when the scratches are gone. I was recently sanding a Lexan windshield for a project and I just couldn't see the scratches that I was trying to remove, even when holding the clear plastic up to the light. It wasn't until I got to polishing the surface that I could see that deep scratches remained in the surface. To get it right I had to go back to stage one and start all over until each successive sanding removed the scratches of the previous sanding. It's a knack that comes with practice unless you just have that skill.

When watching professionals block sand, you will see that they do several things:
1. Start at the roof and work down
2. Block diagonally in both directions (cross cutting)
3. Constantly blow off the sanding dust
4. Wipe with degreaser to see if the scratches have gone
5. Be extremely careful not to rub through around any edges or creases
6. Use tape to protect creases and lines that you want to retain

When you're ready to block sand, give the panel you're working on a light shot of guide coat, typically black, so that you can clearly see the removal of material. A guide coat is applied between each sanding stage and it's important to keep the surface and your sandpaper free of particle buildup, so keep them clear with a blow gun.

Often, Mick or a member of his team will use a material called Like90 Quick Check that is sprayed onto the sanded panel. Quick Check simulates a clear finish and enables the body man to observe any scratches or imperfections in the surface. Any tiny pinholes can be blown clean and filled.

The final stage of the block-sanding process prior to paint is to fill any factory seams with seam sealer. Mick uses a product made by Wurth and uses tape to gain a neat edge to the material. The seam sealer needs to dry before the edges can be sanded smooth.

After many hours of blocking you should end up with a surface, albeit a primer surface, that is as smooth as finished paint. It takes time, patience, and care to achieve that, but a perfectly primered surface will give you a perfect surface on which to paint.

Block Sanding

After the vehicle comes out of the booth, each of the panels to be worked on, in this case the firewall, are given a quick shot of black SEM Guide Coat.

Block Sanding *continued*

Mick usually begins the dry-block sanding process on the roof. Note the variety of blocks used and the tape is there to protect the edges and keep them sharp, there being a tiny crease/swage line in the roof just above the drip rail.

An assortment of blocks, such as these, is available from Dura-Block or your local body shop supply store. Some professionals prefer to make their own blocks.

You can see here that different sanding blocks are used for different parts of the job. This thin block helps prevent rub-through on the inside of the drip rail.

Juan is carefully getting into the corners. Note: the sanding process begins with 150-, then 220-, 320-, 400-, and finally 500-grit. A guide coat is also applied between each sanding.

Here's another shot of that area of the roof that requires very careful sanding so as not to destroy the edge.

When dry sanding, it's important to keep the surface and the sandpaper free of particle buildup. An air line is kept handy for blowing off the dust.

The surface is constantly wiped with degreaser and visually checked for scratches or any other minor imperfections. Note: Never use water on primer, as some primer is extremely porous and do not allow the degreaser to soak in; blow and wipe it off immediately.

Here's what happens when you haven't applied sufficient primer and you rub through to the black primer and beyond. This area can be spot primed. Be sure to use the same primer to avoid witness marks that can be caused by the different drying rates and shrinkage of different primers. That is to say, do not spot it in with a rattle can.

As it was on the roof, masking tape is applied where there is a line in the panel that requires careful attention so that it is well defined and the same on both sides.

Here the rear fender is blocked down to the taped line that will give you a nice sharp edge. In this case, that is where a color change will occur.

A coat of Like90 Quick Check is applied to simulate the depth and clarity of fresh clear on base. It enables the body man to see the shape, highlights, and any imperfections in the paint, and it doesn't evaporate as quickly as degreaser.

Block Sanding *continued*

The Quick Check material gives the primer a glossy finish, enabling the body man to spot any imperfections, as you can see here looking down the rear fender.

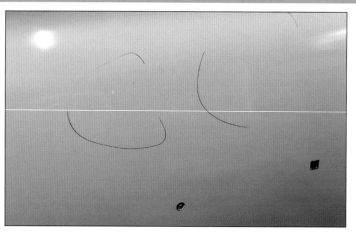

And here they are: two tiny pinholes circled in pencil (not the body trim mounting holes). The pencil lines have to be sanded off, as the paint does not adhere to pencil. Also, do not use permanent marker to mark pinholes, as it will stain the primer and bleed up through the paint. The pinholes should be blown out before being filled.

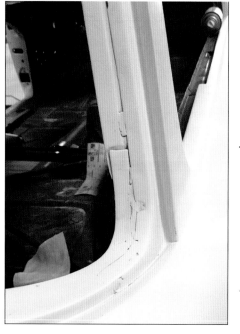

The way bodies were assembled back in the 1950s and 1960s there were plenty of wide seams where panels joined. They need to be filled with seam sealer. The seams are only filled after all the block sanding and sealing is complete, just prior to masking for paint.

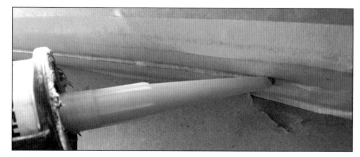

The edges of the seams are first thoroughly cleaned to ensure proper adhesion and then taped to get a nice even straight edge before the gap is sealed using gray Wurth Bond and Seal.

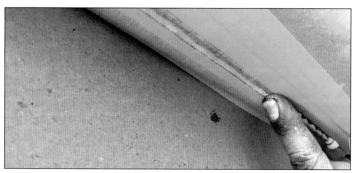

As is often the case with these products, a finger is often the best application tool for spreading the sealer, after which the tape is removed. All working of the seam sealer must be complete before it skins over.

A variety of powerful LED light sources are used to check the entire surface for any pinholes or other imperfections that might cause problems. Those shown are from Scangrip.

Here Juan and Nestor use a couple of lights to check the work on the fender lip. It's an area that the amateur can easily miss from inexperience.

Poncho uses one of the handheld Scangrip lights to check for scratches in the cowl area. It's this attention to detail that separates the winners from the also-ran.

Topcoat

Just prior to the application of color, Mick prefers to give the areas to be painted two light thin coats of PPG DP50LV epoxy primer reduced to "sealer" specifications; that is to say thinned in the ratio of two parts DP50 (50 percent), to one part hardener (25 percent), and one part thinner (25 percent). This is a light, non-sanding primer that aids adhesion between the primer and the paint. Typically, it is allowed 30 to 60 minutes drying time before it is de-nibbed prior to the color being applied.

MATERIALS NEEDED

2–3 quarts PPG DP50LV
1 quarter DPL401LV epoxy hardener
1 quart D8774 thinner

Because this vehicle is tall and mounted on a body dolly, tall and sturdy benches were fabricated and masked to ease the application of sealer on the roof. This helps the painter reach across the roof, not lean on the sides, and concentrate on this one large panel.

After the vehicle is prepped and ready for paint, Mick likes to apply a very thin coat of PPG DP50LV reduced to sealer specs. This is a light, non-sanding epoxy primer that aids adhesion between the primer and paint.

Later, just before it was time to paint the body, the same reduced DP50LV was applied to the rest of the vehicle.

PAINT APPLICATION

If you have followed the guidance so far, you will have a well-prepped project vehicle. There is no need to change your attitude now that it has come time to paint. *Care* and *patience* remain the watchwords, even though we all want to see color.

Unlike many painters, Mick likes to use formulated PPG factory colors that are easy to purchase and fairly easy to match should the inevitable damage occur. That's not to say that you can't or shouldn't go a different route. If this is your first go around, simple makes sense.

It's important that you buy good quality materials; scrimping here could easily lead to problems down the road. Always try to stick to one brand unless you have experience mixing brands of primer and paint and know that it works, as Mick does. Stick to one brand that has been engineered to be compatible across the range.

Buy enough paint. A typical full-size muscle car might require 10 to 15 gallons of paint, clear, and reducer if you plan to paint the engine bay, trunk, and under-floor. For example, you can see in the adjoining chart how much paint was used for Bob Florine's 1957 Ford Del Rio Ranch Wagon, a total of 17 gallons of material for the paint alone

and that's not including primers, etc.

Order it in plenty of time before you begin work. You don't want to be renting space and/or a painter only to find the paint you want is not available. When you have all the paint, be sure to mix it all together so that you have consistent color, including the extra for the inevitable repair down the road.

MATERIALS NEEDED

Note: All quantities are approximate and apply only to this vehicle.

2 quarts PPG DP50LV
PPG 8774 Thinner
PPG DP401LV hardener
2 gallons Aston Martin Bridgewater Bronze
3 gallons Ferrari Avorio
6 gallons of color reducer
1 gallon brown color matched to the interior
5 gallons PPG D8188 Glamour LV Clearcoat
1.5 gallons D8117 Semi Gloss Clearcoat for dash, interior trim, and underside of the body
1.5 gallons of clearcoat reducer

How to Paint

If you've ever watched those TV shows with artists such as Robert Wyland showing you how to paint, you know instantly that you can't do what they do without a lot of talent and practice, no matter how much they explain. Well, painting automobiles is no different than painting whales on walls, it takes skill and practice. If you've never painted a car before, you have a very steep learning curve ahead of you, and if you're determined to go ahead we strongly suggest you enroll in some type of vocational auto body and paint classes, possibly at your local college. You can also try this online at learnautobodyandpaint.com, which is certified by ASE as well as PPG. We also recommend that you visit PPG's Restoration Guide website that has plenty of tips. As my dad would say, "It's not rocket science." However, it is a science and an ever-evolving one as new materials and technologies come onto the market. There is no substitute for practice.

Mick is also of the opinion that you have got to be "in the mood" to paint. It's no good going into the booth facing eight or more hours of hard work if you're not up to it, if you feel a little sick, or if you know you do not have the free time necessary to complete the job. It's a difficult task that needs stamina, concentration, and the freedom to finish the job. If you take your phone in there to take photographs or to make calls during the flash off time, turn it to silent mode. You don't want to be constantly getting calls while you are trying to concentrate. Oh, and go to the bathroom before you get into the booth as you don't want to be opening the door in the middle of the job.

Mick's 25 Tips

1 Mick's first piece of advice is to have a plan. Carefully think through what you are about to undertake. Make certain you have everything you need, from the necessary safety equipment to the materials you need to a phone for taking photos.

2 Buy more paint than you will need so that you have enough to cover the entire vehicle you plan to paint and to have some left over for the inevitable damage.

3 Be sure to mix all of the cans of color you purchase into one batch so that the color is consistent. Typically this is done in a bucket. Be sure to stir up all metallic particles.

4 Be sure to mix enough material to paint the entire vehicle. You do not want to get partway through painting and find out you have run out of mixed paint.

5 Mix your primer, paint, and clear according to the manufacturer's instructions. It used to be that with solvent-based paints when the ratio was two parts paint (50 percent) to one part hardener (25 percent) and one part thinner (25 percent) you could get away with some sloppy mixing. Not so today. The ratios are: two parts paint (60 percent), one part hardener (30 percent), and only 0.1 part thinner (10 percent) now more commonly known as reducer. And note that this ratio doesn't apply to all paints; the manufacturer's

ratios must be adhered to.

6 Before you begin, it is important to set up the gun correctly. It's important to realize that no single spray gun or setup is going to work for your entire project from primer through to clear. For a more in-depth overview, see the gun control sidebar.

7 If you are inexperienced, shoot some test panels so that you can get a feel for it. You can test on some extra masking paper taped to the wall of the booth but do not load up the masking paper on the vehicle.

8 Pre-plan your route around the vehicle, including where you intend to begin painting and where you will finish. You don't want to stop, for example, in the middle of a door. You want to stop at a convenient point at the end of a panel.

9 As you paint, be conscious of the amount of paint you have in the cup so that you don't run out at an inconvenient place, for example, the middle of a door. Remember the paint on the car is drying while you refill the cup.

10 Begin by painting the roof. Mick starts halfway up the sail panel and works his way across the roof to the middle, where he lays on a slightly heavier, wetter coat so that by the time he walks around to the other side it's still wet and the new paint will meld into the old.

11 Remember to do long strokes with the gun and not to overload at the end of each stroke. Experienced painters will "flick off" at the end of each stroke and release the two-stage trigger so that the air is cleaning the nozzle.

12 Plan at the start of each coat to paint the windshield recesses and all the other tricky places such as the door sills, doorjambs, etc., so that you have sufficient paint in those places so as not to color sand through later. This is particularly important with metallics and pearls when you want consistent coverage.

13 It can take 8 to 10 hours to paint a car with base coat and clear, possibly longer, and that just might be the body and not the extra panels and parts, inside, engine bay, trunk, etc. Each coat of your 5 to 6 color coats (and primer for that matter) will take 20 to 30 minutes to apply, maybe longer. Each coats needs at least a 15-minute "flash off" time. Therefore, the time needed to prime or paint your car will be at least four to five hours. In reality, it will take you most of a day.

14 Don't rush. When you plan, plan for the day so as not to find yourself in a crunch without enough time to finish the job.

15 It's important to take everything you need into the booth before you start the job and that includes all the

Mick's 25 Tips

paint materials you're going to need, filters, tack cloth, something to drink, even a book or your phone so that you have something to do during the 15-minute flash off times. You don't want to be opening the door halfway through the job, as the pressure change could suck dust or worse, a fly, in to fall on your job.

16 Most booths cannot be turned off from the inside so as soon as you open the door or have somebody open the door, dust will be sucked in. It's a good idea to have a friend around just in case of an emergency.

17 Stop at the end of each stage (for example, primer or color) and take a rest. It's hot, tiring work. However, do not let paint dry in your gun.

18 It's okay to carefully de-nib after each coat of paint, even metallics, but ideally do not de-nib the last coat of metallic or pearl as doing so could damage the paint.

19 If you should damage the final coat it is possible to dust on some color, but you have to be careful, particularly if you are shooting metallics or pearls.

20 Likewise the clear coat. Just because you're going to flat and polish it, it doesn't mean you can be sloppy. If you get a run, even flatting and polishing might not entirely eradicate it. Repairs are not easy.

21 Even if you're shooting a solid color it's important not to get runs because even after flatting and polishing you can sometimes get a visible line, a "witness mark" in the paint.

22 Gun control is the important issue. You have to be mechanical but smooth and control your speed. For example, if you slow up the paint will be getting thicker, therefore, your speed needs to be consistent.

23 Remember to overlap each and every pass of the gun 50 percent.

24 The gun should always be parallel to the surface you are painting to prevent heavy or light coat striping; however, you will need to tilt the gun to follow the curvature of the surface. Remember if you tilt the gun up, for example, you will get more paint applied at the bottom of the fan.

25 Always allow sufficient drying time. People often rush to see the finished job or to meet a show deadline, but it's important to allow the paint to dry properly. ∎

Mick's Twelve Tricks

Mick has some tricks up his sleeve that might help you achieve your goal of a show-stopping paint job.

▇ 1. First time lucky

If this is your first serious paint job, keep it simple and perhaps go for a one color, single-stage paint job, as it will give you a lot less to worry about. It might even be in keeping with your particular project.

Mick's Twelve Tricks *continued*

■ 2. Cleanliness is next to godliness

Keeping dust from spoiling your paint is essential, so make sure the vehicle is clean and that you are painting it in a clean booth. If possible, mask the vehicle in the booth where you have a controlled atmosphere.

In addition, it is important for your clothing to be clean; even a new suit might not be clean. Mick always checks his suit for particles that might fall into the paint. It gets hot in the booth; Mick typically likes to paint at 80 to 85 degrees F (that doesn't necessarily apply to you) and you might be in there for hours. Strands of your hair will be dislodged and sweat will roll down your neck and arms. To prevent these contaminants from falling into the paint, Mick always wraps his wrists and neck with paper towels.

When you stop painting don't drop your suit onto the floor where it can pick up dust and overspray. Also, be careful when moving the hose around, particularly when you are painting the roof, as the hose can pick up and redistribute dust from the floor. As a precaution, Mick always wraps his hose with clean tape to prevent any previously accumulated overspray from shaking loose and falling into the paint.

Finally, always ensure that your gun is clean. Paint can build up inside the paint passageways, break away, and then fall into the paint.

■ 3. Bridge that gap, clean that crack

Another important point to remember when talking cleanliness is to make certain any sharp body lines are properly clean and dust-free. This will help prevent bridging, which is when the paint wants to bridge across the gap and not go deep into the corner. Bridging can result in problems later.

■ 4. Clean and read the surface

Remember to degrease the vehicle the day before you intend to paint and to tack rag it clean just before you paint. The degreasing stage is actually a good time to "read" the paint. When the degreaser is wet you can look into the finish and see any scratches that have been missed and need to be removed. Also, when you wipe a vehicle down with degreaser, don't allow it to soak in; follow along quickly with a dry rag and a blowgun to dry the surface. This is especially important in colder temperatures.

■ 5. Work in a slight vacuum

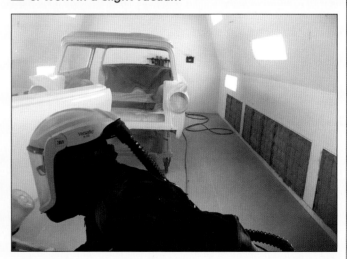

Mick's Twelve Tricks *continued*

Most spraying is performed with a slight vacuum in the booth so that the particulates are exhausted from the booth. The air system is sucking air into the booth from the outside, where there is dust. Make sure the filters are good and that the booth is negative but not overly so. Also, in the case of Mick's booth the filters are doubled up in the middle where the maximum exhausting occurs in order to balance the airflow. Most booths are equipped with a vacuum gauge but it is usually on the outside of the booth, so check before you enter and begin work.

Finally, do not allow anyone to open the door of the booth while you are spraying, as the slight vacuum will suck in dust and possibly insects from the outside. Hang a NO ENTRY sign on the door.

◼ 6. Beware the fly

Flies and other insects are attracted to the bright lights inside the booth, and they will enter when you open the door. They can even be sucked in because of the pressure differential. If an insect drops into the paint, as will inevitably happen, be careful how you extract it; quite often the body will pull away from the legs, leaving them in your paint, and that can ruin all your hard work. It is possible to extract them with a syringe, but whatever you do be careful, especially with metallics and pearls that are difficult to repair.

◼ 7. Agitate and stir

Paint, especially metallics and pearls that contain particles, need to be mixed thoroughly and often. This is a must if you purchased the paint ahead of time and allowed it to sit. Heavy particles settle to the bottom of the can and, if you don't agitate regularly and thoroughly, you can find yourself painting two different colors, one with a lot more particles in it. If you have several cans of paint you must mix them all together and then treat them all the same so that you are constantly spraying the same color.

The same practice must apply on the bench where you are reducing paint and putting it in the gun. The particles must be fully floating so as not to splatter. Something else to remember is that all paint manufacturers have data sheets containing recommended mixing ratios that should be observed. Some experienced painters will deviate, but it is not recommended. Always mix to the instructions.

◼ 8. Have a plan

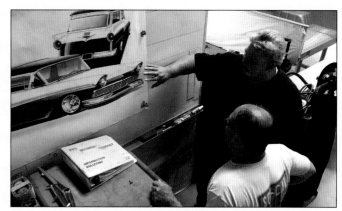

It's imperative that you have a plan or a map of where you will begin to paint and where you will finish. You don't want to overlap and have too much paint on the last panel because you forgot where you started.

◼ 9. Hold the gun correctly

It's all too easy to be careless with the gun and hold it incorrectly, especially if you are new to this. The gun should be parallel to the surface and between 6 and 8 inches from the surface. Be careful when the surface curves so as not to overload that area with paint. Be particularly careful along drip rails and similar areas, as it is easy to get runs in those areas.

10. Count the coats of paint

Counting the coats of paint is very important, especially if you are painting the car with the doors or other panels removed. You don't want to have four coats on the doors and five coats on the body, particularly if you are shooting metallics, pearls, or other custom colors.

It's imperative that you cover the vehicle with the same amount of paint. For example, it's easy to apply too much around the wheel arches, down the edges of the doors, and even along the drip rails. Be careful not to apply too much or even too little paint.

11. Keep it clear

Be sure to apply enough clear coat. If you don't and you later sand through into the paint layer, you will probably spoil your paint job. However, don't be so zealous as to apply too much clear and create runs. While they can be removed, it is very likely you will rub through the clear into the paint and, again, spoil all of your earlier work.

12. A gun finish is okay

In certain circumstances, what is called a "gun finish," that is to say, straight out of the gun and not rubbed down, is acceptable. For example, frames, roll cages, inner fenders, and the pickup bed shown can be gun finish and quite acceptable. A gun finish can save you a lot of time and effort; besides, some of those areas wouldn't have been rubbed out at the factory, it would have been a machine finish. In Mick's opinion, learning to develop a gun finish is good skill development. ■

Gun Control

Before you ever start squirting paint onto your vehicle, it makes sense to familiarize yourself with the gun, just as you would a handgun before you went to the firing range and pulled the trigger. As we suggested elsewhere, if you've never sprayed before it's probably worth investing in a little training, either at your local college or perhaps with a friend who has a paint shop or even your local paint and body store might be able to help you familiarize yourself with the gun and techniques.

Most spray guns, including the SATA 3000 that Mick uses for applying both color and clear coat, have three controls that enable you to adjust the spray pattern for optimum results. Most professional guns will also have an adjustable accessory pressure gauge attached to the bottom of the gun. The three main controls are:

1. The fluid control is the uppermost knob located on the back of the gun. This allows you to adjust the amount of paint that passes through the nozzle by effectively pulling the needle back. Get a basic setting by unscrewing the knob almost completely. Next, pull the trigger back to the fully open position. Then, screw the fluid knob in until you feel pressure against the trigger. This should give you full volume of fluid and a place to start.

2. The fan control is usually a round knurled knob on the side

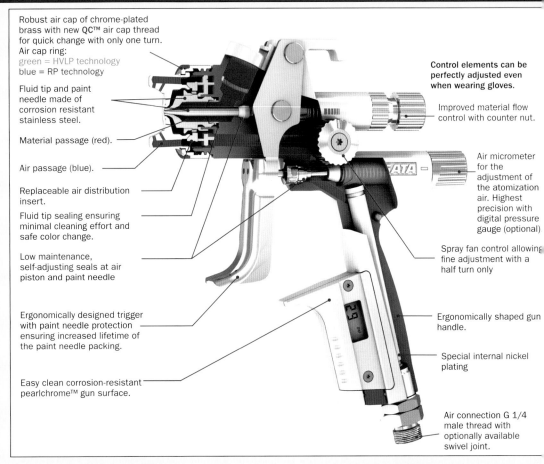

Robust air cap of chrome-plated brass with new **QC™** air cap thread for quick change with only one turn.
Air cap ring:
green = HVLP technology
blue = RP technology

Fluid tip and paint needle made of corrosion resistant stainless steel.

Material passage (red).

Air passage (blue).

Replaceable air distribution insert.

Fluid tip sealing ensuring minimal cleaning effort and safe color change.

Low maintenance, self-adjusting seals at air piston and paint needle

Ergonomically designed trigger with paint needle protection ensuring increased lifetime of the paint needle packing.

Easy clean corrosion-resistant pearlchrome™ gun surface.

Control elements can be perfectly adjusted even when wearing gloves.

Improved material flow control with counter nut.

Air micrometer for the adjustment of the atomization air. Highest precision with digital pressure gauge (optional)

Spray fan control allowing fine adjustment with a half turn only

Ergonomically shaped gun handle.

Special internal nickel plating

Air connection G 1/4 male thread with optionally available swivel joint.

This cutaway is of a SATA gun, similar to the one Mick uses. You can clearly see the three control knobs for fan control, fluid control, and air control. (Photo Courtesy SATA USA)

This SATA jet 5000 is just one of the HVLP spray guns in Mick's arsenal. You can clearly see the knurled knobs used for fluid and air adjustment and the adjustable pressure gauge mounted to the bottom of the handle.

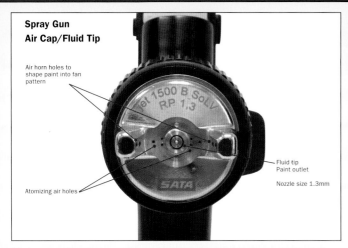

**Spray Gun
Air Cap/Fluid Tip**

Air horn holes to
shape paint into fan
pattern

Fluid tip
Paint outlet

Nozzle size 1.3mm

Atomizing air holes

Every painter has his preferences, but most spray with the pressure set at around 30 psi. Pressure is adjusted using the knurled knob to the left of the gauge.

You can clearly see the needle located in the center of the nozzle, the paint outlet. The small holes on either side of the nozzle are called atomizing air holes. The larger air horn holes force the paint into a fan pattern. (Photo Courtesy SATA USA)

of the gun just above the handle. It controls the amount of air flowing through the gun drawing paint from the cup, dispersing it through the nozzle, and atomizing it. To begin, screw the knob in to achieve a round spray pattern; adjust the shape by backing off the knob.

3. The air micrometer is not found on all spray guns. When there, it is located on the back of the gun just below the fluid control knob; it offers fine adjustment of the air volume and pressure. Usually the air micrometer is in the fully open position.

As mentioned above, begin your gun setup by unscrewing both the fluid control knob and the fan control knob all the way out. This will give you full fluid delivery at the correct air ratio. Next, connect your air line to the gun, set the pressure at 30 psi (that is toward the top end of the green/blue area on the pressure gauge shown), and check the pattern by spraying some masking paper taped to the wall of the booth. That combination should give you a fat oval pattern. You're looking for a nice tall elliptical pattern, so increase the air pressure in 5-psi increments until you get a tall, narrow pattern with a wet center and small even spray at the edges. The correct pattern is achieved by balancing between air pressure and fluid delivery. By screwing in the air control knob, you can adjust the air pressure for improved atomization. This is really a trial and error exercise until you have familiarized yourself with the gun and how to operate its controls. A few passes and you should have the hang of it. ■

The Painting Process

Although ordered in plenty of time, when the paint finally arrived at the eleventh hour it did not match the sample provided (left). If you've rented a booth and/or a painter, this could cause an expensive delay. Make sure you and your paint supplier are well prepared.

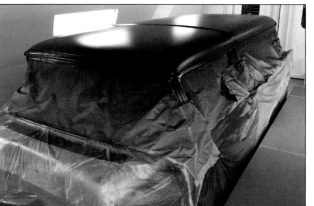

This particular project was to have a two-tone finish; to begin, the vehicle was masked so that the roof could be painted first, allowing the painter to concentrate on this large panel. The color is Aston Martin Bridgewater Bronze.

The Painting Process *continued*

The area below the drip rail was to be another color; however, you can see that it was sprayed along with the roof so as not to get a sharp join line under the drip rail. This area was allowed to dry for 24 hours before it was sanded; water-based paints can be very delicate.

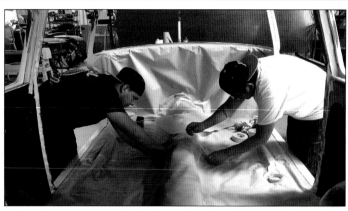

After sanding, the entire vehicle was re-masked for the application of the body color. You have to be careful when masking for the second color to mask the correct areas. It's easy to make a mistake, especially on a tricky color scheme.

Back in the booth with the roof and everything else re-masked, the body is ready for a light coat of PPG DP50LV, which is a light, non-sanding epoxy primer sealer.

The DP50LV aids adhesion between the primer and the paint. The DP50LV is allowed to dry for about an hour before the surface is inspected for any flaws, dust, and so on, and de-nibbed where necessary.

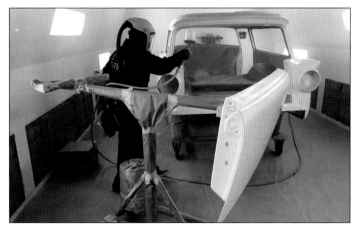

Finally, the color, Ferrari Avorio, goes on: first on the tailgate and then on the body. Because of the timetable on this project, the doors were to be painted along with the inner fenders. Note: In all cases, Mick mixes all of the cans of paint together for a consistent color. This is a basic but essential process.

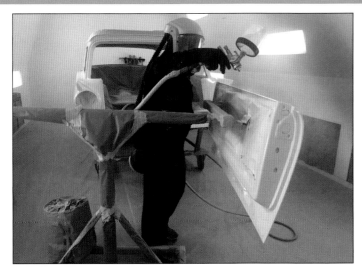

After the 4 to 6 coats of color have been applied and allowed to dry for 20 to 30 minutes, two coats of PPG D8188 "Glamour" Clearcoat are applied to protect the ivory color, which is very susceptible to damage from dust and fingerprints at this stage in a two-tone scheme.

Once the two coats of clear had been applied from the roof down, the vehicle was left to dry overnight. If you're renting a booth, make sure you plan for this.

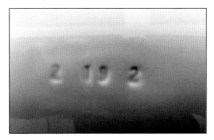

If you're looking for authenticity and possibly trying to meet a judging criteria, certain identification numbers might need to be left intact.

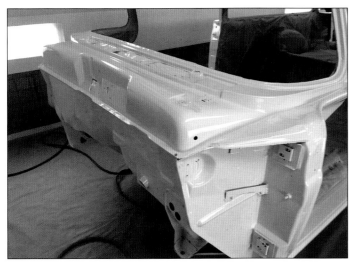

Note how during the painting process the firewall caught up with the rest of the car and now matches the body color.

After two coats of clear were applied to protect the ivory and allowed to dry overnight, the whole vehicle was wet sanded using 800-grit paper.

It's imperative that you use a good quality rubber sanding block for the wet sanding process and not resort to using your fingers, as that will only leave grooves in the surface. Mick prefers well-made 3M sanding blocks.

Masking for Second Color and/or Graphics

In the case of the 1957 Ford Del Rio Ranch Wagon followed here, it was to have a two-tone paint scheme. Everything below the drip rail was painted ivory that would then be oversprayed where necessary with bronze. That might appear to be a waste of some time and materials but in Mick's opinion it is more efficient time-wise to approach it that way than to mask a lower edge for the ivory and then come back and re-mask an upper edge for the bronze.

In order to achieve that effect, the ivory was first given two coats of clear coat for protection. Why? Because as you are working on masking the lower bronze portion, you don't want fingerprints, glue, or any other substance to mark the ivory, and the clear coat will protect it. It was then wet sanded with 800-grit paper before the color split was laid out. It's important to note that when Mick masks an edge like that in the color split, he uses 3M Vinyl Fine Line Tape for the separation. He then masks up to the Fine Line using regular tape and paper. The reason for this is that the vinyl tape does not have the small wrinkles that regular tape has and there is less chance of paint creeping under the tape. Subsequently, the area not to be painted bronze was masked and the vehicle put back in the booth.

Masking for Second Color and/or Graphics

Here you can see where the graphics are being laid out with 1/4-inch masking tape. Note how the color break was positioned to be hidden under the side trim.

Mick carefully measures the color break across the back. The conical shape of the taillight housings causes an optical illusion, and getting it right is critical.

After making a cardboard template of the decklid trim, Juan carefully positions it in the center of the tailgate and marks it accordingly.

All is right and the color break and the decklid trim are in perfect alignment. Time to mask for the application of the second color.

Masking for Second Color and/or Graphics *continued*

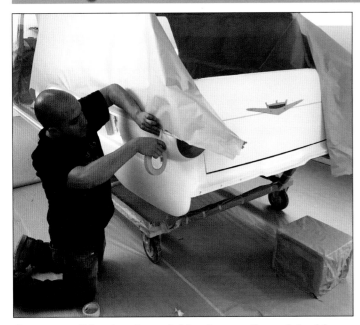

Once everything has been laid out correctly and double-checked for accuracy, Miguel masks the middle of the wagon, which will remain ivory. It's actually Ferrari Avorio.

When taping for a color separation or for graphics, Mick uses 3M Vinyl Fine Line Tape. It doesn't have the slight wrinkles of regular masking tape; therefore, there is less chance of paint creep.

You can see here where the Vinyl Fine Line Tape is used to mark the color separation while regular masking tape and paper is used for the main area to be masked. Then, there is less chance of damaging the paint line when you are removing the masking.

Second Color

In the case of the second color, in this instance Aston Martin Bridgewater Bronze, it was applied after the ivory had been allowed to dry overnight. The next day, the vehicle was carefully sanded wet with 800-grit. The entire surface was then thoroughly cleaned and degreased prior to the vehicle getting its second color.

Applying Second Color

The second color, in this case Aston Martin Bridgewater Bronze, is being applied to the bottom half of the vehicle.

Applying Second Color *continued*

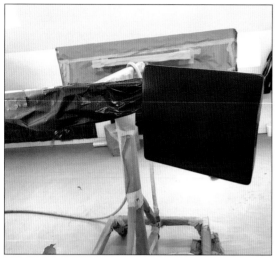

Note the gas flap was sprayed with the car but not on the car so that the painter could paint the filler recess in the body.

Note: The gas cap is sprayed in the same vertical position as it would be on the car, as are the doors and fenders. This is particularly important with metallics and pearls in order that the particles in the paint align.

The masking is removed while being very careful to pull the tape back over itself to reduce the risk of the paint peeling off with the tape. Note: Water-based paints peel off easily if not treated with care and they are difficult to repair if damaged.

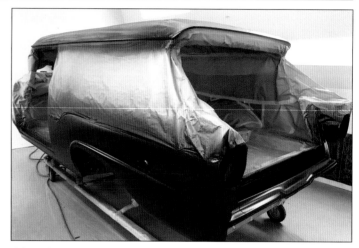

After the second color was applied, it was allowed to dry for 20 to 30 minutes. The longer the dry time the better, depending upon the type of paint; water-based paints are quite delicate compared to acrylic paints.

The PPG clear coat system Mick's Paint uses consists of D8188 Glamour LV, D8774 compliant reducer/ thinner, and D8384 medium hardener.

It's starting to look pretty cool. The clear was allowed to dry for a couple of weeks before it is really ready for wet sanding.

After the unmasking, the area below the drip rail was given five to six coats of clear. At this stage any marks buried under the clear will be exaggerated. Any contaminants will be forever trapped under the clear.

Roll Cage

If, like Ed Chalupa's 1967 Ford Fairlane, your car has a welded-in roll cage (most sanctioning bodies no longer allow bolt-in cages) now is the time to paint the cage. It's a tricky, time-consuming but feasible operation that, in this case, had to be done after the main paint. Ideally, you would paint or powder coat the cage after fabrication and mock-up. The joints of the tubes would then be ground clean so that the cage could be installed and welded in place, leaving only the welded areas to be touched in.

Roll Cage Painting

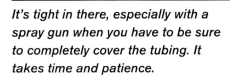

You can see that the entire car has to be masked off before the roll cage can be painted.

Up close you can see from inside the trunk that it's quite an exacting task to make sure everything is masked and that none of the black roll cage paint gets onto the rest of the car.

It's tight in there, especially with a spray gun when you have to be sure to completely cover the tubing. It takes time and patience.

Painted and unmasked, the roll cage, shown here from inside the trunk, looks professional, race ready, and legal.

It looks equally good from outside the car, but, again, maybe it would have been preferable to paint the cage outside the car and then assemble it inside before touching-in the welds.

Rules and Regulations

It used to be that you just hooked a spray gun up to Mom's vacuum cleaner and, *voilà*, the car had a shiny new coat of paint for the weekend cruise. It was a long way from the days of Henry Ford's quote, "Any color you want as long as it's black." However, those days are likewise long gone since the 1963 Clean Air Act passed to control pollution. There were major amendments to the Act in 1970 and again in 1990. In a nutshell, every county in the United States should have regulations governing the refinishing of motor vehicles. If your county does not have regulations then you should refer to the state regulations.

After a brief conversation with a representative of the South Coast Air Quality Management District (SCAQMD) that governs air quality in the counties of Los Angeles, Orange, Riverside, and San Bernardino, I Googled auto painting regulations in Michigan and immediately came up with a government site. This site explains, in fairly understandable language, what the regulations are for Michigan. Incidentally, Michigan offers a free help line: (800) 662-9278. I assume you can do the same for your state.

In Los Angeles, where this book was written, we are governed by SCAQMD Rule 1151, "to reduce volatile organic compound (VOC) emissions, toxic air contaminants, stratospheric ozone-depleting compounds, and global-warming compound emissions from automotive coating applications performed on motor vehicles, mobile equipment, and associated parts and components."

One cannot argue with the fact that we need to protect our planet and that painters need to protect their health. So, no matter where you live, I suggest you get on the Internet and acquaint yourself with the regulations governing your county. Or, talk to your local auto paint store or paint rep.

Rule 1151 is technical in the extreme, and even after several readings I remained perplexed. As noted above, I subsequently contacted the SCAQMD (listed in the Source Guide) where a representative was very helpful explaining that in essence you basically have to meet the VOC content limits indicated in the attached table and that those specifications should be on every can of paint.

All automotive paint materials should carry a label such as this that lists the volatile organic compounds. In this case, the actual is 218 grams per liter, whereas the regulation is 271 grams per liter.

TABLE OF STANDARDS

VOC CONTENT LIMITS		
Grams per Liter of Coating, Less Water and Less Exempt Compounds		
AUTOMOTIVE COATING CATEGORIES	**Current Limit**	
	g/L	Lb/Gal
Adhesion Promoter	540	4.5
Clear Coating	250	2.1
Color Coating	420	3.5
Multi-Color Coating	680	5.7
Pretreatment Coating	660	5.5
Primer	250	2.1
Single-Stage Coating	340	2.8
Temporary Protective Coating	60	0.5
Truck Bed Liner Coating	310	2.6
Underbody Coating	430	3.6
Uniform Finishing Coating	540	4.5
Any Other Coating Type	250	2.1

CUSTOM FINISHES

A Brief History

When the hobby of hot rodding and customizing first got started prior to World War II, there really wasn't any so-called custom paint. Of course, two-toning had been popular since the early part of the 20th century, but only basic colors were available until the early 1920s when General Motors began to work with DuPont to create new automobile pigments called Duco. These nitrocellulose lacquers, known simply and collectively as lacquer, were introduced in 1923 at the New York Auto Show. Meanwhile, General Motors started a color advisory service, sending researchers to auto shows to ask people what they'd like to see on the palette. And, in 1927, Harley Earl headed up GM's, and indeed the industry's, first Art and Color Section.

Lacquer was a vast improvement over what had preceded it, but it dried slowly and was very susceptible to gasoline. Experimentation continued, and in 1929 the first alkyd enamel paint appeared. It was tougher than lacquer, dried faster, resisted gasoline, and could be applied without the need for compounding.

Despite the economic climate, paint chemists continued experimenting with ever more wild creations, adding first herring scales and then metallic particles, primarily aluminum, for ever brighter colors. The first factory metallic paint appeared on the 1929 DeSoto. Unfortunately, the metal was heavy and would separate from the carrier. While these new colors were simple (maroon, green and blue) they did not hold up well; nevertheless, the public and the custom car crowd especially lapped them up.

The real explosion of color came after WWII as a consequence of rapid technical developments during the war effort and returning soldiers who had money to spend on automobiles. At the time, there was a fledgling underground hot rod and custom car scene but all that changed when

Before there was custom paint as we know it, there was two-tone, even from the factory. Mick's Paint gave the duo-tone look to Greg Shubin's 1952 Buick Special using a combination of black and GM Mosport Green.

SCAQMD Rule 1151, (18)

METALLIC/IRIDESCENT COLOR COATING means any automotive coating that contains more than 0.042 pounds per gallon (5 grams per liter) of metal or iridescent particles as applied, where such particles are visible in the dried film.

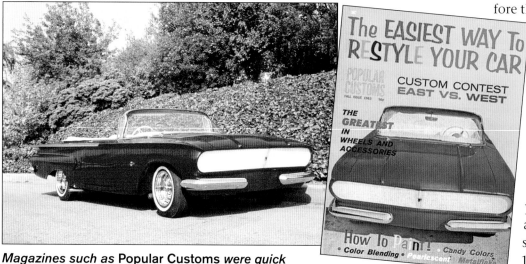

Magazines such as Popular Customs *were quick to publicize the new trends in custom paint materials and techniques, spreading the word not only nationwide but also internationally. The actual car on that cover of* Popular Customs *from the fall of 1963 was a full custom 1960 Chevy convertible painted at Barris Kustom.*

Robert E. Peterson published the first *HOT ROD Magazine*. Launched in January 1948 at the inaugural Hot Rod Exposition, *HOT ROD* changed the hobby forever, giving it an international voice proclaiming there was now something else to do with your car other than race it and that was show it. For some, finish became as important as speed. Indeed, the Barris brothers, George and Sam, advertised "Custom Auto Painting" in the first issue. Barris was soon followed by others including Jimmy Summers, Al Wallace, and Link's Custom Shop. A custom paint industry ever in search of something new was off and running.

By the October issue, Ditzler, a division of PPG since 1928, was

Pinstriping goes back to Egyptian times and is still used to decorate horse-drawn carriages as well as custom cars. Here, master striper Dennis Ricklefs stripes the hubcaps of Bruce Wanta's Troy Ladd–built 1936 Packard Roadster.

advertising "Custom Colors for Custom Cars," listing first four and then by December, six paint distributors in the Los Angeles region. Even though these paints were available, not everybody could afford them; cheaper and more accessible methods of custom painting surfaced. For example, pinstriping came to the

fore through the efforts of Kenneth "Von Dutch" Howard, the so-called Originator of Modern Striping.

Dutch took the traditional striping used to embellish fenders, body moldings, and hubcaps and turned it on its head with free form, surrealist striping. In the early-1950s, having your car "Dutched" became a big fad, especially when he striped a 1927 Studebaker for 10 straight days at the 1955 Pan Pacific Auditorium Motor Review show.

Experimentation was the name of the game and painter George Cerney developed what he called "Easter Egg" colors when he added a drop of color to white primer. Colored primers were quite popular for some time. However, in northern California, Mel Pinoli, who operated Pinoli's Body and Paint Shop in San Leandro, California, was playing with translucent toners, trying to find the secret to what would eventually be called

What looks simple is usually tricky to accomplish. Planning the order in which these Martini-style stripes were applied was quite a task. (Photo courtesy Didier Soyeux)

Candy Apple, a name coined by customizer Joe Bailon because they looked like a candy apple you'd get at the fair. Pinoli tried printer's ink, and it worked for a while but faded after a few months. Meanwhile, in Los Angeles, Jesse Lopez, who worked at Barris Kustom, likewise tried different combinations of clear and toner until he hit on the right combination for his brand-new 1958 T-Bird.

In 1956, acrylic enamel superseded alkyd enamel and changed the game again, offering much improved durability and a wider range of bright, pleasing colors including metallics. There was also now a clear coat that could be used to protect the base color from sunlight. It was also needed to "bury" and protect the metallic particles.

In 1957, Dow Chemical purchased the Dobeckmun Company that introduced the custom car world to Metalflake in 1959. The vehicle was George Barris's XPAK400 hover car that, according to the accompanying press release, "Contained a million particles of chromed aluminum called 'Metalflake.'"

XPAK400 debuted at the New York World's Fair and was quickly followed by a cover story in the February 1961 issue of *HOT ROD*. The cover blurb read: "Customize your car with 3rd dimension color." Alongside were printed impressions of the NEW SPARKLE PAINT. Featured in the article was Dick Scritchfield's freshly maroon "flaked 1932 Ford roadster." Metalflake set the custom car world aglow and it has not looked back.

Metallics and Metalflake in particular need a lot of clear to not only carry the particles but also to protect them from overzealous compounding; rub through and the flake is ruined. Consequently, in the late-1960s, paint chemists developed mica particles coated with titanium dioxide that act like a prism, both reflecting and transmitting light and giving a much brighter and more versatile effect compared to reflective flake. The use of mica initiated myriad colors and effects that revolutionized the custom paint industry; an industry that continues to experiment and develop new products, new techniques, and new and exciting finishes.

People couldn't resist touching it when they first encountered Metalflake. Multiple coats of clear protected the flake seen here on a 1960 Chrysler.

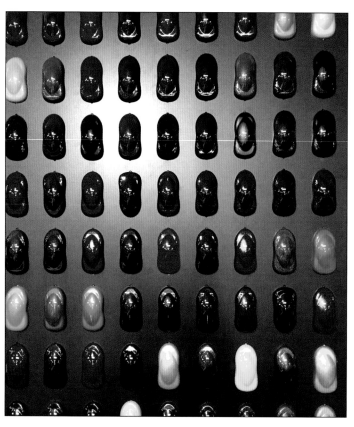

As you can see in any good paint store, there are simply hundreds if not thousands of colors available to today's custom painter. So different from the early days of hot rodding and customizing and Henry Ford's "Any color you want as long as it's black."

Mick's Philosophy on Custom Paint Finishes

For a number of reasons, Mick is not a fan of custom paints. His biggest problem is that they are usually difficult to match when you are not painting a car all at once, a situation that occurs all too frequently at Mick's Paint. However, his biggest reason for disliking custom paint finishes is the difficulty of repairing them.

"All too often cars get damaged," Mick said. "It's the nature of the beast, and satisfactorily repairing any type of custom paint that is not formulated is always an issue. Sure, it can be done, but in my world, I prefer not to do it. My preference is to use formulated factory paint, factory colors that, if all things are equal, can be fairly easily matched. To me, it just makes sense.

"I have also found inconsistencies in custom colors where two cans of the same color do not match. If that's the case and you damage the paint, it's almost impossible to match in a cost-effective way. A door ding, for example, might result in repainting the whole side of a car, and if it's candy you need a real expert to be able to blend it.

"There's an amazing array of factory colors available now to choose from, for example, Randy Ito's 1955 Chevy Cameo pickup. I can't tell you how many people have asked if that's candy blue, but it's actually a factory Toyota color used primarily on the Prius.

"James Austin's 1955 Chevy truck was beautifully painted by Gary Howard, but when a piece of flying debris badly damaged the truck, Gary had no formula for us to follow, he had just mixed a cool color that was

PPG is always Mick's first choice. It offers a wide range of custom colors in its Radiance, Harlequin, Prizmatique, and Flamboyance selections.

PPG Prizmatique blue No. 190413 goes over a silver metallic base No. 36577 and shows an exciting range of colors as the light reflects from the surface.

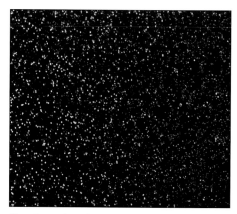

On the other hand, Prizmatique light silver No. 36579 over a black base No. 95060 gives and entirely different effect.

Looks like a candy finish, but Mick actually painted the late Gene Olsen's 1951 Merc convertible using a factory Ford blue.

With no formula to follow, James Austin's 1955 Chevy truck, beautifully painted originally by Gary Howard, had to be almost completely repainted by Mick's when it was damaged.

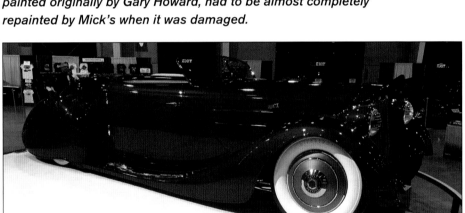

Looks like custom-mixed paint but actually the color on Bruce Wanta's Troy Ladd Hollywood Hot Rods–built 1936 Packard Roadster Mulholland Speedster is a factory color good enough to be America's Most Beautiful Roadster in 2017.

almost impossible to match. Consequently, we had to repaint almost the whole truck.

"Look at Bruce Wanta's 1936 Packard Roadster built by Troy Ladd's Hollywood Hot Rods. It won America's Most Beautiful Roadster Award and yet it's a factory color. If it got damaged, I know I could repair it.

"I would never paint a car of my own using a custom color. My advice to is cruise your local car lots on a sunny day and look at all the wonderful formulated factory finishes that are available, everything from metallics to pearls, and pick something that is formulated and repeatable anywhere in the world, especially if this is your first foray in the world of custom paint.

"I would say if you are going to use an off-the-shelf custom color

The late Larry Watson popularized the panel paint–style exemplified here on Billy F Gibbons's 1958 Mexican Blackbird. As striking at the car is, it's a clever yet simple combination of black and House of Kolor Lime Gold Pearl over a white base. (Photo Courtesy Alex Maldonado/ Blacktopsociety.net)

On a trip to the Goodwood Festival of Speed in England, Billy F Gibbons's CadZZilla was so badly damaged it had to be completely repainted at Mick's. Originally it was House of Kolor. Mick got as close as possible to the original paint using a black base and a custom mix of pearls. (Photo courtesy Randy Lorentzen)

KAMELEON™ KOLORCHANGE FLAKES

Wild holographic ultra-thin flakes to spur your imagination. Available in two sizes: 1/64th and 1/128th. Shown over BC-25 Black Base

F-27 Yellow Lime Flake	F-28 Kamen Blue Flake	F-29 Fools Gold Flake	F-30 Violet Red Flake
F-31 Rich Gold Flake	F-32 Fireball Flake	F-33 Fine Rainbo Flake	F-34 Pink Rose Flake
F-35 Emerald Green Flake	F-36 Sea Blue Flake	F-60 Mini Yellow Lime	F-61 Mini Kamen Blue
F-62 Mini Fools Gold	F-63 Mini Violet Red	F-64 Mini Rich Gold	F-65 Mini Fireball
F-66 Mini Pink Flake	F-67 Mini Emerald Green	F-68 Mini Sea Blue	

If you want to go the custom paint route, we strongly suggest that you mix together all the cans of paint so that you have a consistent color. Also, make sure you have enough for any repairs necessary down the road.

then begin by mixing all the tins of paint into one so that you have consistency. And, make enough so that you have spare paint for any inevitable repair."

Custom Paint Types

There are now many types of custom colors available to the auto painter, everything from traditional metallics to the latest low-gloss pearls. Here is an overview of the basics.

Candy Apple

True candy apple is created in a three-step process:

1. A reflective base, usually gold or silver metallic but also white or even black
2. A transparent colored "candy" layer
3. A protective clear coat

As light shines on a candy finish it passes through the clear coat and candy layer to the base, where it is reflected back through the candy and clear coats. This approach creates truly unique car paint colors. The downside of candy finish is that it is more expensive, more difficult to apply, and certainly more difficult to repair.

Color Changing

These automotive paint colors change color based on the viewing angle between the observer and the light source. Like candy paints, color changing paints are a three-stage process. However, they usually employ a non-reflective base, for example, black.

1. A non-reflective base such as black
2. A color changing pearl
3. A protective clear coat

As with candy paints, color changing paints are difficult to apply and repair, and they are much more expensive than conventional automotive paints.

Low Gloss or Matte

Low-gloss or matte finishes can be achieved in a number of ways:

1. A high epoxy content primer coat
2. A high PVC content in the paint coat itself
3. A flattening agent in the clear lacquer coat

Typically a low-gloss finish is achieved with a three-stage process: base, color, and low-gloss clear; however, you can actually get low-gloss single-stage paint.

Metallic

Metallic finishes are usually very small flakes of uniform-sized aluminum suspended within the paint. The particles reflect light, giving the paint a sparkly metallic effect that does not change color when viewed from different angles.

Typically, metallics would consist of a two-stage process that is a base coat containing the metallic particles and a protective clear coat.

Pearl

Primarily mica based, pearl paints reflect, transmit, and refract light, acting like very small prisms that refract white light into different shades. Pearls can be two-, three-, or even multiple-stage systems.

FINISHING THE JOB

While a lot of work has been achieved in getting the body and all of the panels painted, the job is far from over, particularly if you are painting a show car. There is the underbody to do and all painted areas have to be color sanded.

Out of Sight, but Not Out of Mind

You might think it is not important to worry about the underside of your car, but if you intend to enter any kind of show, somebody is bound to take a look and see what you did or didn't do down there. In the case of muscle cars coming out of Mick's Paint, they are nearly always, unless the owner specifies otherwise, finished to a high standard. They are protected with Smart bed liner material, coated in body color, and finished with low-gloss clear coat for protection. As with everything connected to the task of properly painting a car, this is just as time consuming and laborious, but it has to be done.

It's also a difficult task if you do not have easy access to the underside of the car. For example, you can see that Mick uses a hoist to lift the body well clear of the ground so that his team can work underneath. You might have access to a rotisserie for this task, but if not you're going to struggle.

Assuming you are in a position to spray the underside of the floor pan, be conscious that when sprayed, the bed liner material goes everywhere and you will need to mask the surrounding area. The material can be brushed or rolled on for a little more control and less mess but at the price of possibly an uneven finish.

One thing to note is to make a decision as to whether the wheelwells are to be body color or black. Body color can look strange and accentuate any dirt that later accumulates in the wheelwell. It might, therefore, be better to go black.

Materials for Underbody

Note: All quantities are approximate and apply only to this vehicle.
2 x 1 gallon kits of Smart bed liner black
0.5 gallon PPG DP50LV sealer
0.5 gallon of color
0.5 gallon of color thinner
1 gallon satin clear coat
0.25 gallons clear coat thinner

Underbody Painting

For most people, getting to the underside of the project is not going to be as easy as working on this hoist, which affords maximum access.

Underbody Painting *continued*

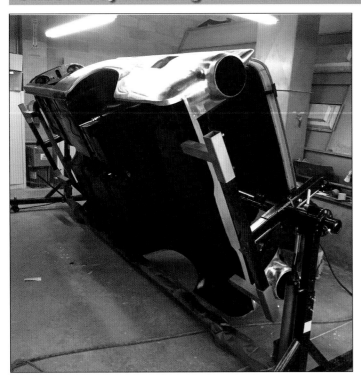

If you don't have a hoist, perhaps you have access to a rotisserie. Regardless, you will have to get underneath the car to sand the black primer sealer.

As on the topside, all the seams were filled with Wurth gray seam sealer, and the same applies on the underside. Obviously, the sealer needs to be smoothed out before it can be oversprayed.

Once the whole underside has been sanded, it needs to be cleaned and degreased with PPG One Choice degreaser. It's a laborious, backbreaking, neck-bending task.

When the underside is ready, the vehicle is lowered so that everything can be masked. When sprayed, the bed liner material goes everywhere and needs to be contained as much as possible.

Mick always uses Smart truck bed liner from FinishMaster. It's 50-state compliant and applied with a Schutz gun, roller, or brush (for different results). Two 1-gallon kits were used here.

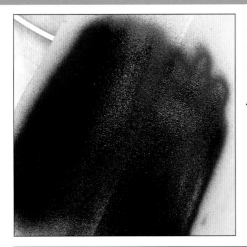

Mick always shoots a test before spraying the actual project just to make sure the texture is as desired. A brush or roller can also be used.

A Schutz gun is used to apply the Smart truck bed liner material. You can see here how the surrounding area was well masked to protect from overspray.

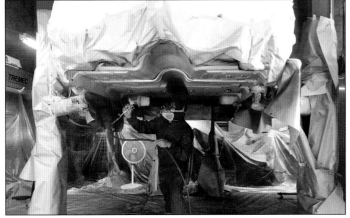

After the bed liner material has been allowed to dry overnight, it is given a good coat of PPG DP50LV primer sealer. The primer needs to dry for 20 to 30 minutes, and you might use a different DP if you were going for a lighter color of paint.

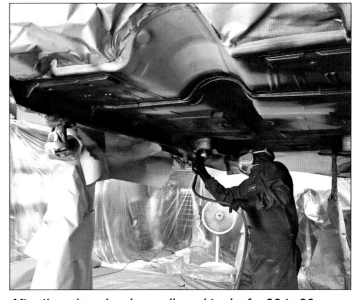

After the primer has been allowed to dry for 20 to 30 minutes, the body color is applied. Note how the painter is careful to get material into all the little nooks and crannies.

Once the whole underside of the vehicle has been painted the body color, it is protected with a low-gloss clear coat. Note that sometimes the wheelwells look better black than body color.

Color Sanding

The final color sanding process is just as important as every preceding stage and, like everything before it, it takes time and patience. For a top, show-quality finish, Mick insists on a well-lit working environment, preferably fluorescent lights that will enable you to see any scratches. Also, he keeps the doors closed to prevent dust and grit from blowing onto the surface.

Mick always uses good quality sanding paper, such as that from 3M; cheap papers can be inconsistent especially in the 3000-grit ranges. He begins with 1000 wet-or-dry and works patiently through 1200, 1500, 2000, 2500, and finally 3000. He always uses a block; sanding with your fingers and no block will create an uneven surface that will be magnified when buffed, exactly the opposite of what you're trying to achieve. It's also good to soak the paper for about an hour in clean water before you begin sanding.

He always uses a good-quality sanding block such as those from Snap-On, as cheap blocks can have ridges at the edges that cause scratches or uneven sanding. He insists on using fresh soapy water as a lubricant. The water and the sponge have to be clean so that there is no harmful grit that can scratch the paint. If you drop the sponge in the dirt, throw it away or at least wash it thoroughly before you use it again on the paint.

Something to remember is to keep track of time so that you can finish a panel in each grade of paper before stopping. This will help ensure that you don't sand the same area twice with the same grade paper and inadvertently remove too much material. Also, don't start sanding a panel unless you know you have time to finish it. Finally, remember you have to be extremely careful with this process; there's no room now for errors and a rub through. Great care is required. You can begin to see why a top-class paint job costs so much.

Color Sanding

The color-sanding operation takes place out of the booth so that the booth can be used for other projects and to keep it dry and free from dirt. Also, keep the workspace door closed to prevent dust and grit from getting blown onto the project. Note that the tall benches are utilized to reach the roof and large banks of fluorescent lights are used to illuminate the working area.

The final color sanding is a long and time-consuming job, starting with 1000-grit wet-or-dry and working patiently through 1200, 1500, 2000, 2500, and finally 3000 and always with a block. Miguel is using lots of clean, soapy water as he sands in opposite directions. Cross cutting ensures you will be getting it flat. Mick reckons they will typically make 100 passes with each grade of paper from 1500-grit and finer.

Color Sanding *continued*

Good quality sanding blocks, such as those from 3M that Mick uses, are essential for attaining a flat surface. Some cheap blocks can have ridges at the edges.

Miguel employs a variety of different size and shape blocks in order to negotiate the various contours of the hood in order to keep it flat.

Extra care is needed in areas such as this around the gas filler and where you have a bodyline behind the masking tape so as not to rub through. It's important to squeegee dry the areas, checking as you go for scratches.

Not so critical on the fender here but on the rest of the car you should be conscious and careful of where the dirty water gravitates. It may be difficult to clean up.

Great care must be taken on areas such as the rear window frame or similar. Notice that even here Miguel uses a rubber block inside the 2000-grit paper.

Buffing

If anything, the buffing process is more critical than the sanding process because you now have equipment involved. If you've never done this before, there is the potential for things to get out of hand. When you're hand sanding, you should have a little more control. If this is your first time, get an old panel to practice on because its very easy to destroy the paint with careless buffing. For example, you should always use two hands to hold the buffer and you should keep it constantly on the move to prevent the pad from getting too hot and scorching the paint. If you have access to air-powered buffers, note that they stop more quickly than their electric counterparts.

You should always tape the easily damaged edges, such as the drip rails, where you can inadvertently buff through. Any tricky areas should be buffed by hand, especially if you are inexperienced.

As we recommended with every-thing from stripping to painting, always begin at the top of the vehicle and work your way down. Remember to cover the finished panels, such as the roof, when they are completed. If left, the compound can attack the paint and leave marks that you have worked so hard to remove.

In summary, Mick employs a simple system, and it works. At each stage of the buffing process, he removes all of the marks in the paint before he moves on to the next step. This is not a time to rush.

Buffing the Paint

Mick exclusively uses 3M Rubbing products decanted into an easy-to-use bottle in the following order: 1: Rubbing Compound No. 05974

2: Finesse-It II Machine Polish No. 05928
3: Machine Polish No. 05996

For buffing, you're going to need a large polisher such as this 7-inch Makita 9227 (0 to 3,000 rpm) electric polisher. It has a preset speed setting dial (from 600 to 3,000 rpm) for maximum control. Typically, the compounding speed should be between 600 and 1,500 rpm.

It's also important to buff away from the edges; you should have the pad spinning away and not toward an edge as the pads can easily catch.

For the first compounding/buffing stage, Mick employs a Schleger lamb's wool pad part No. H175-0 with 1.5-inch pile used in conjunction with 3M Machine Polish No. 05974. Note: The lamb's wool pad is more abrasive than the foam pads used subsequently.

Always use two hands because, believe it or not, the lamb's wool easily catches. Keep the pad moving at an even pressure, as it can generate heat and burn the paint. Note: Miguel uses two hands and is careful to keep the cord over his shoulder and out of the way of scratching the paint.

For the smaller, more difficult areas to compound, small polishers such as this air-powered tool from Chicago Pneumatic are used in conjunction with 3M buffing pad No. 85078.

Juan uses a small air-powered polisher to polish the top of the fender of the 1967 Fairlane. Again, note how he keeps the air hose out of reach of the vehicle.

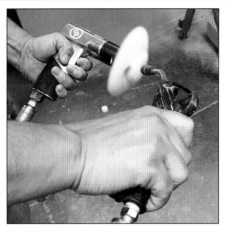

It's important to keep the pad clean and free of compound buildup, so every once in a while an air gun can be used to blow the pad clean.

For the second compounding stage, Mick uses the white pad part No. 05723 with the Finesse-It II polish No. 05928. The final buffing is accomplished with the gray 3M-pad part No. 05738 and rubbing compound No. 05996.

The final compounding is done with the gray pad and the rubbing compound No. 05996. Obviously, great care is taken not to rub through.

Here Miguel uses another air-powered polisher. This one is fitted with a foam pad to polish the tight areas around the drip rail. Great care is needed for these operations.

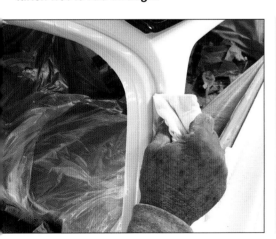

After the main areas have been mechanically polished, Juan goes back in to address the areas the mechanical polisher can't get to or is unsuitable for.

As always, hidden inside the polishing cloth is a rubber block to prevent finger marks that will only be exaggerated when polished.

Mick also employs these Kirkland Signature ultra high pile premium-detailing cloths. He has removed the tag so that it doesn't scratch the paint.

Assembly: What's on First?

It almost goes without saying that when it comes time for assembly you need more of the same requirements that got you to this point: time, patience, care, space, and a plan. Unless you have a show deadline, which is sometimes good to force the project to a conclusion, taking some time to assemble your project is paramount to a happy conclusion.

Often as not in the show car world, time is what you don't have. Cars get painted, and worse upholstered, way too late in the process; therefore, assembly has to be rushed, mistakes get made, details get omitted, and worse, things such as paint get damaged. It's not the way to get 'er done. Far better to stand back, take a deep breath, and make a plan as to how this is going to come together in a timely, caring fashion. That said, it's great to have a deadline to work to.

What's to plan? Just put it together, right? Wrong. To begin, think about the order in which the car has to go together. Even the mere task of making a list will help you remember things that need to get done. For example, as in the case of the wagon shown here, the brake lines needed to be secured to the frame before the body went on because they run between the body and the frame. Likewise, the wiring; think about where that is going to run. Wait, before you even put the body on, do you have the body mounts and correct bolts? Have you got all the trim pieces and clips? Are the instruments ready to be installed in the dash? Who's on first?

You also need to consider how many friends you're going to need because hanging doors, fenders, and hoods especially are tasks that require more than one man, sometimes two or three, because the last thing you want to do at assembly time is damage the paint you've spent so much time getting right.

Assembly is a massive, daunting task that needs a lot of careful consideration before you launch into it. Make a plan, make lists, get things prepared and pre-assembled, and take your time.

Final Assembly

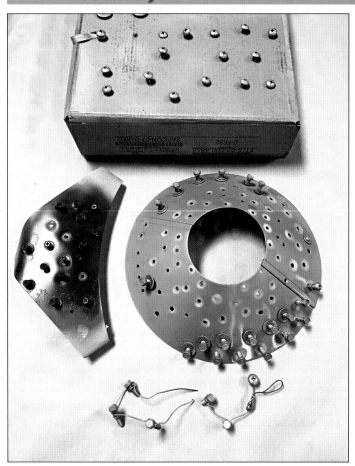

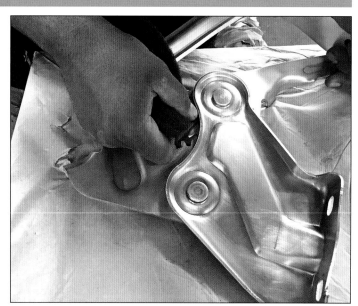

Small parts such as the hood hinges can also be prepped and ready for installation. Don't forget to gather the correct hardware and any necessary shims.

Before you begin assembly, you can begin gathering and preparing all of the hardware ready for installation. Typically, Mick's uses ARP Racing Products, sometimes stainless steel, and sometimes the nuts and bolts are painted to match, as seen here.

Final Assembly *continued*

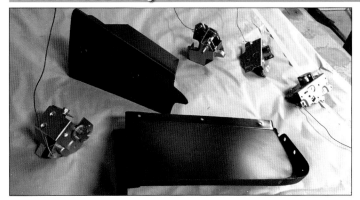

Likewise door latches that have been painted in semigloss silver and small metal covers were shot in semigloss black.

Do not work on a surface, even if it's a blanket, that is covered or impregnated with metal chips; they will destroy all of your hard work.

A clean piece of carpet remnant is a great surface on which to assemble your project, as it will protect your knees and any parts that you may accidentally drop.

Owner Bob Florine (left) and Steve Strope of Pure Vision Design review the assembled chassis about to go under the body. Note the brake lines are installed. The wheels are just rollers.

The engine for the wagon is a stack-injected, all-aluminum, 520-ci Boss Nine built by John Kaase Racing Engines. It produces 770 hp and 730 ft-lbs of torque with a hydraulic roller cam. The engine color is a custom mix by Pure Vision Design using PPG materials.

It's a tight fit so the stainless headers, fabricated by Ace'D Auto WorX, were installed on the Boss before it was dropped into the frame. It's procedures such as this that need thinking through before you ever lift a wrench.

Final Assembly *continued*

First order of business on Bob's wagon was for Steve Strope of Pure Vision Design to install the brake lines, as it would be impossible to install them after the body had been lowered onto the chassis.

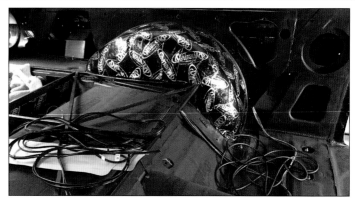

Dynamat sound and vibration suppression material was installed throughout the vehicle prior to the installation of the complex wiring system.

The door striker that had already been prepared by blasting and painting was installed using new ARP hardware.

If your doors were painted off the car, as these were, you're going to need one or two friends to help you hang them. However, be aware that if you removed the body from the frame, it could bolt down slightly askew and put the doors out of alignment. Some adjustment might be necessary.

As you can see, even the tailgate hinges were pre-painted and, as with the door hinges, had their threads tapped clean before being carefully installed.

The trim was being fabricated and installed as the vehicle was being assembled. You might want to get as much of the interior as possible pre-assembled.

In the case of Bob's wagon, the doors were stretched. Rick Lefever had to stretch the door sill plates, which required buying four and making two by welding the oh-too-thin anodized aluminum strips together.

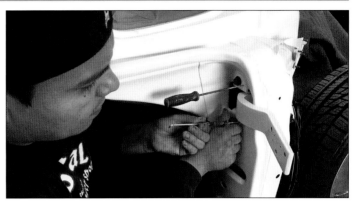

Something Poncho always does is drill tiny guide holes in the hinges so that they can be installed in exactly the same position as they were when the body was blocked.

Poncho and Miguel began installing the front sheet metal, including the inner front fenders. Note: The inner surface is painted with black Smart bed liner material to make the surface disappear. Body color would have been too bright.

Installing fenders can be a two- or three-person job, so make sure you have some friends at this stage to give you a hand.

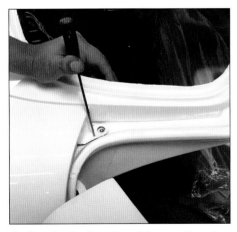

As he did for the door hinges, Poncho pre-drilled guide holes for perfect re-alignment of the fenders.

A close up of the guide holes drilled to align the front fender, the inner fender, and the radiator support panel. This may seem like a lot of work, but it will save you a lot of time and trouble.

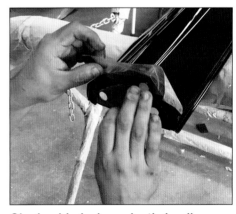

Single-sided, clear plastic leading-edge aircraft tape available from AircraftSpruce.com was used to protect the paint-to-paint surface between the fenders and the cross bar.

Final Assembly *continued*

The cross bar takes two to install, as it needs to align with the fenders and somebody needs to hold one end while somebody else installs hardware at the other.

If you are using stainless steel bolts such as these from ARP, a little anti-seize will prevent galling and aid in both installation and removal.

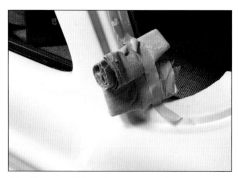

Until everything is buttoned up, painted areas that might get easily damaged, such as tailgate and backlight, should be protected.

Likewise, any orifices, such as the injector stacks and the fuel filler neck, were covered to prevent dropping the odd clip, nut, or bolt down there.

The splash apron was installed after the cross bar. Notice that Ivan wears protective glasses when he is working upside down.

A fine array of stainless steel fasteners from Automotive Racing Products helps the appearance of the underside.

Installing the trim is also a two- or three-person job, especially if it's multi-piece like the wagon's trim. Here Rick and Mick protect the paint with tape while they trial fit the trim.

The first three pieces are installed, which took most of a day to accomplish correctly. Incidentally, the trim is original stainless steel but chrome plated.

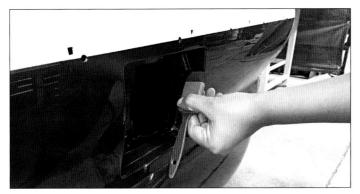

A small stiff brush was used to clean out any compounding residue left in the seams. For example, here in the gas flap or around the drip rail. Note that the paintbrush is wrapped in tape so that the metal banding does not scratch the paint.

Miguel gives the wagon a quick wax with Meguiar's Gold Class to protect the surface before the car leaves to go back to Pure Vision Design for final assembly.

Mick and Miguel go over the entire vehicle with keen eyes to look for any minor blemishes before it gets returned.

A final inspection revealed this small amount of buffing compound lodged under the inside of the drip rail. Other places to look include doorjambs and cowl vents.

Final Assembly *continued*

The residue was easily removed with a brush, again with the metal band taped to protect the paint, and some cleaner.

Here's some of what you're looking for and what took the time; the super-straight highlight that runs along the top of the door and fender. Getting that straight is where all the hours went. Note: The doors were extended so all that tapered, curving trim had to be fabricated to fit and look factory.

Likewise, the highlights in the roof caused by the reflection of the fluorescent tubes show how flat and straight the roof is.

Proud of their work, the crew (from left to right) Ivan, Juan, Miguel, and team leader Poncho, get ready to bid adios after almost a year together.

Protectionism

Mick never actually washes any of his cars or projects. Rather than wash them, he begins the cleaning process by blowing off any surface dust with a rubber-tipped blowgun. He then gives the surface a light dusting with a lamb's wool duster. These are available from a number of sources, including The Home Depot, and Mick suggests you regularly shake the duster to remove any debris. Finally, when the surface is dust-free, Mick uses a Kirkland towel and a quick detailer, for example Meguiar's, to wipe down the surface. After that, he adds a coat of good wax and the job is done. Mick's process, which has served him well for many years, couldn't be simpler.

Mick refuses to wash any of his show-class paint jobs; instead, he insists on using a rubber-tipped blowgun to blow away any dust that has gathered on the vehicle.

Once all the surface dust has been blown off, Mick lightly dusts the paint surface with one of these lamb's wool dusters that he prefers over the impregnated dusters.

After the dusting, Mick uses any brand of quick detailer or waterless wash and a Kirkland towel to wipe down the surface.

After a wipe down with waterless wash or quick detailer, Mick uses clean Kirkland towels to wax the surface, typically with Meguiar's Gold Class.

Source Guide

A&M Sandblasting
9344 Oso Ave., Unit D
Chatsworth, CA 91311
818-727-1865
sandblasting@att.net
In-shop sandblasting service

Ace Automotive Cleaning Equipment
401 N. Griffin St.
Grand Haven, MI 49417
616-392-9090
888-772-3263
ace-sandblasting.com
Soda blasting equipment

Ace'd Auto Worx
6085 King Dr., #106
Ventura, CA 93003
818-631-1969
acedautoworx.com
Custom exhaust fabrication

Alsa
1213 E. 58th Pl.
Los Angeles, CA 90001
800-999-4120
info@alsacorp.com
alsacorp.com
Manufacturers of custom paints,
including chrome finishes

Aircraft Spruce & Specialty
225 Airport Cir.
Corona, CA 92880
877-477-7823
951-372-9555
aircraftspruce.com
Aircraft supplies, including paint stripper
and tape

American Classic Cars
2282 Arrow Hwy.
La Verne, CA 91750
909-596-5700
cmt2000@verizon.net
amclassiccars.com
Classic car sales

Applied System Technologies
9800 W. Kincey Ave.
Suite 135
Huntersville, NC 28076
704-947-6966
appliedsystemtech.com
Aluminum piping

Automotive Racing Products
1863 Eastman Ave.
Ventura, CA 93003
805-339-2200
arp-bolts.com
Manufacturers of precision fasteners

Auto Air Colors
14 Airport Park Rd.
East Granby, CT 06026
800-243-2712
autoaircolors.com
Manufacturers of water-borne custom
paints

Auto Body Tool Mart
2545 Millennium Dr.
Elgin, IL 60124
800-382-1200
info@abtm.com
autobodytoolmart.com
Auto body tools, equipment, and
information

Auto Source Today
autosourcetoday.com
Online and quarterly printed catalog of
auto body equipment

Best Buy Automotive Equipment
844-383-4167
951-297-9044
bestbuyautoequipment.com
Nationwide distributors of body shop
equipment, including rotisseries

Cal Blast
687 N. Benson Ave., Unit C
Upland, CA 91786
909-949-9505
calblast.com
Media blasting specialists

California Dustless Blasting
16529 Sierra Hwy.
Canyon Country, CA 91351
888-DUSTLESS (CA Location)
800-285-9834 (Outside CA)
californiadustlessblasting.com
Mobile blasting service

Carcoon America
5570 Florida Mining Blvd. S., Unit 101
Jacksonville, FL 32257
866-910-0899
carcoonworkstation.com
Inflatable workstations

Central Pneumatic/Harbor Freight
800-444-3353
harborfreight.com
Nationwide tool distributors

Chicago Pneumatic
cp.com
Industrial manufacturer of power tools,
air compressors, etc.

Collision Services
P.O. Box 599
1050 Dale Dr.
Hudson, IA 50643-0599
800-367-6575
collisionservices.com
Auto body and paint supplies

Composition Materials
249 Pepes Farm Rd.
Milford, CT 06460
800-262-7763
compomat.com
Media blasting materials suppliers

Custom Painting Pearls
770-858-5575
custompaintingpearls.com
custompaintingpearls@yahoo.com
Manufacturers of custom paints and
pigments

Didspade
480-588-6355
didspade.com
sales@didspade.com
Internet distributors of custom paints
and pigments

DNA Custom Paints
5–7 Keith Campbell Ct.
Scoresby, Victoria 3179
Australia
61-3-9764-2088
dna-paints.com
Manufacturer of custom paints

Dura-Block
6324 S. 199th Pl., Ste. 101
Kent, WA 98032
253-854-0090
dura-block.com
Manufacturer of sanding blocks and
other finishing tools

Dustless Blasting
5711 Schurmier Rd.
Houston, TX 77048
800-727-5707
713-868-8041
dustlessblasting.com
Suppliers of dustless blasting equipment

Dynacorn International
4030 Via Pescador
Camarillo, CA 93012
805-987-8818
dynacorn.com
Manufacturers of replacement body
panels and complete bodies

Dynamat
3042 Symmes Rd.
Hamilton, OH 45015
513-860-5094
technical@dynamat.com
dynamat.com
Manufacturers of acoustic solutions

FinishMaster
4809 Holt Blvd.
Montclair, CA 91763
317-237-3678
888-311-3678
finishmaster.com
Nationwide manufacturers and distributors
of automotive and industrial paint

Eastwood Automotive Tools
263 Shoemaker Rd.
Pottstown, PA 19464-6433
610-323-9099
800-343-9353
eastwood.com
Tools and equipment

Eastwood Automotive Tools
12100 S. Cicero Ave.
Alsip, IL 60803
855-286-4046
800-343-9353
eastwood.com
Tools and equipment

Eastwood Automotive Tools
5673 Ridge Rd.

Parma, OH 44129
866-483-2258
800-343-9353
eastwood.com
Tools and equipment

El Camino College
1111. E. Artesia Blvd.
Compton, CA 90221
310-900-1600
compton.edu
Auto body and paint education

Evercoat Metalworks
6600 Cornell Rd.
Cincinnati, Ohio 45242
513-489-7600
evercoat.com
Manufacturers of body shop finishing
materials including plastic-repair materials

Gabe's Custom Interiors
24215 Ward St.
San Bernadino, CA 92410
909-884-5150
gabescustom.com

Custom upholsterers
Louis M. Gerson
16 Commerce Blvd.
Middleboro, MA 02346
508-947-4000
800-225-8623
gersonco.com
Manufacturers of tack rags and related
body shop products

Henkel Adhesives North America
henkel-adhesives.com
Manufacturers of adhesives and surface
preparation materials

Icengineworks
6085 King Dr., Unit 106
Ventura, CA 93003
818-631-1969
aron.crawford@icengineworks.com
icengineworks.com
Exhaust and headers manufacturer

Klean Strip (WM Barr)
P.O. Box 1879
Memphis, TN 38101
800-398-3892
kleanstrip.com
Paint removal chemicals, solvents, etc.

Learn Auto Body & Paint
learnautobodyandpaint.com
Online training

Like90 Products
10 Greg St., Ste. 162
Sparks, NV 89431
775-358-0422
888-954-5390
like90.net

Manufacturers and distributors of body
shop products

L&M Stripping
14232 Aetna St.
Van Nuys, CA 91401
818-983-1200
lmstripping.com
Specializes in chemical stripping

Andrew Mack & Son Brush
216 East Chicago St.
P.O. Box 157
Jonesville, MI 49250
517- 849- 9272
mackbrush.com
Manufacturers of pinstriping and
cleaning brushes

Meguiar's
17991 Mitchell St. S.
Irvine, CA 92614
800-347-5700
meguiars.com
A division of 3M; manufacturers of
car-care and refinishing products

MetalWorks Paint and Rust Removal
1182 Bethel Dr.
Eugene, OR 97402
877-412-8806
metaldipping.com

Mick's Paint
1359 E. Grand Ave., Bldg. B
Pomona, CA 91766
310-947-6727
mick@danieljoseph.com
mickspaint.com
Specialists in automotive restoration and
refinishing

Metalflake
7 Arrowhead Cir.
Rowley, MA 01969
508-932-3339
metalflakecorp.com
Manufacturers of custom paints

Miller Electric
1635 W. Spencer St.
P.O. Box 1079
Appleton, WI 54912-1079
920-734-9821
millerwelds.com
Manufacturers of welding equipment

Paint With Pearl
2709 Saint Paul St.
Denver, CO 80205
303-725-9637
matt@paintwithpearl.com
paintwithpearl.com
Manufacturers of custom paint materials

Patton's
3201 South Blvd.

Charlotte, NC 28209
704-523-4122
pattonsinc.com
Industrial air compressor distributor,
fabricator, and supplier

PCL Automotive
3150 E. Pico Blvd.
Los Angeles, CA 90023
800-672-4900
pclautomotive.com
Manufacturers of primers and refinishing products

Pennsylvania Warehouse
456 Riverport Dr.
Leetsdale, PA 15056
724-251-9960
Manufacturers of replacement body
panels

Powermate
800-628-8815
airservices@powermate.com
powermate.com
Manufacturer of generators and air
compressors

PPG
19699 Progress Dr.
Strongsville, OH 44149
800-647-6050
autorefinish@ppg.com
us.ppgrefinish.com
Manufacturers of refinishing materials

Quincy Compressor
701 N. Dobson Ave.
Bay Minette, AL 36507
251-937-5900
877-784-6292
quincycompressor.com
Manufacturers of compressors

Scangrip A/S
Rytterhaven 9
5700 Svendborg, Denmark
45-63-20-63-20
scangrip@scangrip.com
scangrip.com
Manufacturers of professional LED
lighting solutions

SEM Products
1685 Overview Dr.
Rock Hill, SC 29730
866-327-7829
cust_care@semproducts.com
semproducts.com
Manufactures auto body shop products

South Coast Air Quality Management
21865 Copley Dr.
Diamond Bar, CA 91765
909-396-2000
aqmd.gov
Government air-quality agency

Strip Clean
5105 W. 1st St.
Santa Ana, CA 92703
714-775-7797
Chemical stripping services

Uline
12575 Uline Dr.
Pleasant Prairie, WI 53158
800-295-5510
Uline.com
Masking supplies

U-POL US
108 Commerce Way
Stockertown, PA 18083
610-746-7081
610-743-8654
sales-us@u-pol.com
u-pol.com
Manufacturers of fillers, coatings,
aerosols, adhesives, and paint-related
products

Urekem
38 S. Park Dr.
Perkinston, MS 39573
601-928-5197
877-583-0040
urekem-paints.com
Manufacturers of custom paints

U.S. Chemical & Plastics
600 Nova Dr. SE
Massillon, OH 44646
330-830-6000
800-321-0672
uschem.com
Manufacturers of auto body chemicals,
fillers, etc.

U.S. Paint
831 S. 21st St.
St. Louis, MO 63103-3902
314-621-0525
uspaint.com
Manufacturers of custom paints

Wheeler Speed Shop
17662 Metzler Ln.
Huntington Beach, CA 92647
714-842-1881
wheelersspeedshop.com
Custom car and hot rod builder

Wurth USA
93 Grant St.
Ramsey, NJ 07446
201-825-2710
800-987-8487
wurthusa.com
Manufacturers of body-shop chemicals

Zendex Tool
4 Larson Dr.
Danbury, CT 06810
203-778-0400
zendextool.com
Manufacturers of GoJak